GREAT CANADIAN
Fishing
STORIES
THAT DIDN'T GET AWAY

*For Del Lawredeuer,
In the hope that you
might appreciate life is
comprised of more than
little white balls.*

*Only the best,
Dale Brin
May 10/02*

**Edited by
David E. Scott**

The Publisher: Lone Pine Publishing
206, 10426-81 Avenue
Edmonton, Alberta
Canada T6E 1X5

202A, 1110 Seymour Street
Vancouver, British Columbia
Canada V6B 3N3

16149 Redmond Way, #180
Redmond, Washington
USA 98052

Canadian Cataloguing in Publication Data

Main entry under title:
Great Canadian Fishing Stories

ISBN 1-55105-118-4
1. Fishing—Canada. I. Scott, David, 1939-
SH443.G74 1997   799.1'0971   C97-910342-8

Layout and Design: Tammy Anderson
Cover Design: Rob Weidemann, Black Dog Design
Printing: Best Book Manufacturers, Toronto, Ontario, Canada

The publisher gratefully acknowledges the support of Alberta Community Development, the Department of Canadian Heritage and the Canada/Alberta Agreement on Cultural Industries.

ACKNOWLEDGEMENTS

Thanks to the contributors without whom this anthology wouldn't exist!

I cheated a bit in the selection process since humour is different things to different people, and acknowledge with thanks the kind efforts of my informal selection committee who handicapped the mass of material from which the gems within these covers were chosen. Take a bow Joan Nichol of Ailsa Craig, Ron Blackman of London and my infinitely supportive wife, Wendy.

Thanks also to Brian Bowman, Editor of *Western Sportsman*, Regina; LaVerne Barnes, Tourism British Columbia; Helen Jean Newman, New Brunswick Economic Development & Tourism; Gerard Makuch and Wendy Gold, Saskatchewan Tourism Authority; Jack Davis, Peterborough, Ont., Executive Director of the Outdoor Writers of Canada; Martin Hintz, Milwaukee, Editor, *The Travel Writer* of the Society of American Travel Writers; James Rainey, State College, Pa., Executive Director, Outdoor Writers of America; Lorraine Williams, Willowdale, Editor, *Maple Leaf Rag*, of the Canadian Chapter, Society of American Travel Writers.

-DES

EDITOR'S NOTE

The Canadian government began phasing in the metric system of measurement in 1971, and by now most Canadians have at least an approximate idea of the length of a kilometre or the weight of a kilogram.

Canadian sports fishermen, however, continue to catch fish in pounds and ounces. They still measure the really big ones with their hands spread wide–in feet and inches. And when they cast a fly into that black, foam-flecked pool at the base of the rapids, it's a 40 or 50 foot cast, not 12.2 metres or 1,524 centimetres.

Since anglers have never been concerned about scientific precision in their stories, strict accuracy in reporting the length and weight of fish, the height of their jumps and the distance of their runs, is not adhered to in these pages. This is, after all, a book written by fishermen, about fishermen, for fishermen. Or, as the government that brought us the metric system would have it, by fisherpersons, about fisherpersons, for fisherpersons.

- DES

INTRODUCTION

It starts with a hook and a length of string tied to the end of a tree branch or sapling. If the kid gets hooked, he or she graduates in time to a real fishing rod with a real reel on which to store real fishing line. The lures progress from worms and grubs found under rocks to sophisticated mechanical lures on swivelled steel leaders.

If the ardour intensifies, funds are always found to lower the odds with expensive boats and the space-age aids of sonar, radar and instant digital printout thermometers. Others eschew scientific aids and become purists. Standing crotch-deep in ice water they spend thousands of hours learning to cast a piece of fluff into the wind onto a target area the size of a dinner plate.

Though fish may get caught in the process, it's the anglers who get hooked!

The kid now catches his first rock bass on a designer-labelled, TV-touted fishing kit, but the game is the same. That first tug on the line, signalling the presence of a hungry or curious fish, starts the adrenalin flowing. Many never permit those adrenalin rushes much surcease, making fishing the most popular sport worldwide and the only truly international sport whose devotees are governed only by the gaming regulations of where they wet their lines.

This anthology is dedicated to those who are hooked and who live for this most solitary but most companionable pursuit. They may pursue it with equipment that could have retired their mortgage, dressed in elegant designer togs; they may dress as disreputably as hoboes and hunt their quarry with hand-me-down dime-store junk. Their angling techniques are as varied as the fish they chase.

But they all share the same grand passion, and their excuses and justifications for its unremitting pursuit are as earnest and devious as those of the alcoholic.

It was Pete McGillen, writing in the old Toronto *Telegram* in the 1950s, who offered us one of the most succinct justifications: "If you're too busy to go fishing, you're too busy," Pete wrote.

Every angler–grand master or dabbler–will read about himself or herself in many of the vignettes in this unique national collection.

When you anglers have had your chuckles, consider passing this book along to your non-angler spouses, companions or relatives. (Better yet, buy them their own copy!)

Perhaps it will help them understand why you prefer rain down your neck, blackflies up your nose, ice water in your waders and a fish-hook in your thumb . . . to the warmth of their company and the comforts of home.

Then again, it may not.

David E. Scott
Ailsa Craig, Ont.
1995

CONTENTS

A FISH A MINUTE
By Lyn Hancock

Who says fishing is boring?

I did . . . but that was before I cast a line in the water for the first time and caught my first fish–a sixteen-pound Arctic char!

I had not flown to Bathurst Inlet Naturalists' Lodge for the fishing, though most do. I was intent on more exciting pursuits–like trudging the tundra to capture on film musk ox and caribou, wolves and foxes, climbing the cliffs to watch peregrine falcons feed their young, boating upriver to photograph incredible waterfalls.

But on this particular day, on a trip to a creek a few miles south of the lodge, my companions, Troy, 7, Robbie, 9, and Tim, 11, insisted on fishing. They had come north to fish and that was what they were going to do.

Their guides were 19-year-old Sam, an Inuit, and Boyd, 15, the son of lodge director Glenn Warner.

Troy's father, George Gibson, a doctor from Yellowknife, Robbie and Tim's grandmother, Nancy Stride, from Toronto, Roger, a ski-trip director from Vermont, and I just went along for the ride.

Sam and Boyd dropped us off where Fishing Creek entered the inlet. In the lightened boat they would negotiate the fast-moving, shallow waters of the river while we meandered to the lake to meet them.

The boys' rods were in the water almost as soon as they reached the boat.

"Okay, you three," said Roger, "we'll go look for wolves while you fish." And then to the guides, "What time will we be ba--?"

10:00 a.m.: A scream rent the air. "I've got one!" Before Sam could get to the boat for a landing net, tiny, seven-year-old Troy had managed to land a fish almost as long as he was–a ten-pound lake trout. Dr. George told me later that his son, a veteran of northern fishing trips, was probably the only kindergartener to take a ten-pound Arctic char to Show and Tell.

I dived for my camera and, acting like a Hollywood movie director, started shouting instruction.

"George, I want to take a picture." Always cooperative, George looked up and grinned cheerfully. "George, not you. I want a picture of your son. Troy, push the cap away from your face. And don't look so pained. It can't hurt that much."

Poor kid; there was no time to click the shutter.

10:01 a.m.: "Robbie's got one!" Nancy yelled. "And it's big."

Everybody rushed to the water. There was Robbie reeling in a second lake trout–all 12 pounds of it.

"Come and get in the picture," I shouted, ecstatic about two big fish. Sammy grabbed Troy's fish, Boyd grabbed Robbie's fish, and I composed a photo of two little kids struggling to lift their prizes onto a handy set of caribou antlers.

There was no time to focus.

10:02 a.m.: "Tim's got one!" his grandmother called. "And it's even bigger."

We turned to look, and there was Nancy's second grandchild straining against what turned out to be a 14 pound lake trout.

I could hardly believe it. Three young boys all under 12 with three fish almost the same size as they were. Staggering under the weight of their fish and spurning the help of their guides, the three youngsters lined up for my camera.

10:03 a.m.: I was focusing when George yelled, "I've got one too!"

The kids dropped their trophies to run to the shoreline and offer verbal support.

"Come on, Dad, you can do it!" Troy encouraged.

"Easy Dr. Gibson, don't reel it in too hard," Tim chimed in.

"Keep your rod tip high," Robbie suggested.

The rod tip was high, forming a very tight arc. Crack! The rod snapped under the pressure, and the fish swam free.

10:04 a.m.: There was no time for commiseration. Roger had made an ideal cast and was now fighting a 10-pounder. He landed it and decided, "I don't need it; let's put it back." Dr. Gibson gently worked the hook free, moved the fish back and forth to force water over its gills, and we watched it swim away.

"Your turn, Lyn," Boyd said, pushing his rod at me.

"Me? I can't fish. I don't even like fish. I'm scared of them."

I fought back the memories of squeezing myself deep into the bow to avoid the slithering, flopping piles of snapper my father insisted on bringing into the dinghy. Of running down the street in terror away from gleeful neighbourhood kids chasing me with slimy mackerel. Of forcing myself to axe off the heads of goggle-eyed cod before I could fillet them to feed seals and seabirds in my care. I had come to the Arctic for animals, and that didn't include fish. I was trapped. "I don't know what to do," I protested.

"I'll show you," said 15-year-old Boyd. "It's easy."

"Okay," I agreed reluctantly, "but just one cast."

Boyd told me what to do, and with beginner's luck, the lure flipped out into the river. I started reeling it in. One cast would be enough to show the kids I was a good sport.

"Faster," ordered Troy, the seven-year-old.

I obliged–all the sooner to go birdwatching. "Oh! It's hit bottom. There, see what I've done. I've caught the bottom."

"No! You've got a fish," shouted Robbie, the nine-year-old.

"Don't be silly," I answered, sensing a thrill of fear. "It's a boot." In these pristine waters?

"No! It's a char!" yelled Tim, the 11-year-old. A sliver of pink and green knifed the water. "Hold onto it! Don't lose it!"

Suddenly there were no more awful, fishy memories. I wanted only to hang onto the moment–and the fish.

"Nancy! Grab the camera. Take a picture."

The line was heavy with fish; it stopped coming in. I dug in my heels.

"Keep winding," commanded Boyd, as Sammy, a smile on his face, stood by with the landing net.

"I can't turn it!" I moaned, enclosing all of the reel's bale in my hand, desperately trying to inch the line around the spool. The pressure was terrific. "It's going to break the rod."

"Keep it high!" That was Dr. George.

"Nancy! Haven't you got a picture yet?" I pleaded, trying to turn to see if she had located my camera among the lake trout, caribou antlers, hiking gear and other equipment scattered around her feet.

"Which one?" she asked.

"Use both of them!"

"Here Roger," Nancy commanded, passing the buck and the camera to him, "you take them. I'm only used to instamatics."

Later Roger was to say I was totally out of control. Nancy was sorting cameras and lenses. Roger and George were clicking shutters as cameras were handed to them. Boyd continued patiently instructing me on how to bring in the fish. And Sammy? Sammy waited quietly, probably quelling internal hysterics at the antics of the white man.

The kids pranced up and down, more excited about my fish than their own. And I was straining backwards in an agonizing position with the end of the rod pointing back into the air behind my back.

The char was heavy and fighting strong. I dug in my heels and tried to pull the rod around so I could wedge the butt-end against my chest and take some of the strain off my aching fingers. I felt that at any moment I would lose the rod, the char and my new-found interest in fishing.

"Have you got a picture?" I yelled at the patient photographers.

"A picture?" Roger yelled. "We've got 20 of them; how many more do you want?"

They say that after I stopped swearing to the entire heavenly family, I babbled: "The rod's going to break. I can't keep it high. It's going. I can't move the bale. It's fixed. The fish's fixed it. The char's still there? My father won't believe this. He came to Canada and said there were no fish. He didn't get one."

"You're not going to either, if you keep your eyes on us," my audience hollered. "Keep your eyes on the fish."

Then at last. The reel ran free, and I could wind again. It kept on winding, and the ripple far out in the water soon surged into a wave at my feet. Sammy scooped up for my close inspection a sixteen-pound Arctic char.

My Inuit friends carefully wrapped it in plastic and heavy cardboard and tied the package with rope so I could carry it on the plane. It did look a bit like a rifle when I boarded the jet to fly south from Yellowknife, but the flight attendants were kind; they kept it in the galley when I found it wouldn't fit under my seat.

I mean, surely they didn't expect my first fish to be that small?

Lyn Hancock is an award-winning freelance writer and photographer and author of a dozen books including *There's A Seal In My Sleeping Bag, There's A Raccoon In My Parka, Love Affair With A Cougar, An Ape Came Out Of My Hatbox, The Mighty Mackenzie, Tell Me, Grandmother, Northwest Territories, Alaska Highway* and *Looking For The Wild.* She lives in Fort Simpson, North West Territories, and Mill Bay, British Columbia.

TEACHING ALBERT
By Marty Roberts

Learning to hunt and fish can be a wonderful adventure. If you were taught by the right people, as I was, you will experience a lifetime of pleasure, relaxation and inner peace. When someone opens the proverbial window on nature, you discover a great new world. Now it is time for our generation to pass on this private pastime and admit our children into the membership of the sacred organization of lovers of the outdoors.

This was the speech I was prepared to give to the young lad whom I had agreed to instruct in the fine arts of hunting and fishing. I decided that I should start Albert with a weekend fishing trip. I picked him up on Friday night, and we set out on our six-hour drive to the lake. Somewhere within the first twenty miles, Albert snored so loudly I couldn't hear myself talk.

"What are you honking at?" he asked as he crawled back onto the seat from under the dashboard. "There isn't another car in miles."

"Oh, sorry. There was a chipmunk on the road," I said, trying to ease him into lesson one. Originally I was determined not to teach lessons but to let him experience the trip as a whole.

"Albert, the first thing you have to learn is the camaraderie of the trip," I said. "You have to get to know your partners. Since you don't have any trips to talk about, I'll tell you about mine." Although we arrived at our destination before I finished all my tales, I did manage to cover from age eight to 19. Perhaps I'd have a chance to bring him up to the present on the return trip.

"What's it like to ride in the back of the truck?" Albert wanted to know, removing bits of cotton from his ears.

I must admit I was proud of the enthusiasm Albert exhibited scrambling from the truck, but he soon met his first block. "Where's this fancy cottage you're always telling me about?" he wanted to know.

"Oh, I rented that to some friends. We'll have much more fun in the tent."

I gave Albert the choice of pitching the tent or gathering firewood. He said he wasn't hungry and would really like to try out the back of the truck. Boy, what a kidder! We got the tent up and our supper half warmed before the rain started. It was nice of Albert to share a couple of his candy bars with me; they seemed to ease the indigestion from the brittle spaghetti.

The next day went smoothly. The sun was bright, the fish were biting, and Albert and I enjoyed each other's company. Seeing three of my favourite lures plunge to the bottom of the lake inspired me to instruct Albert on how to tie proper knots for fishing. And right about the time the water rose to his shoelaces, Albert understood the function of the old tin can he'd taken out of the boat and thrown in the back of the truck.

As Albert hauled in his fifth fish, he became curious as to why I wasn't catching any. I said I was too busy watching him to concentrate on my own technique. As we were coming off the lake, I was thinking that we had really had a good day. We had got through it without throwing each other in the drink, and we had five nice fish between us. That brought to mind another lesson for Albert. No matter how many fish were caught or who caught them, they became "ours." I told him that the terms "we" and "us" should almost always be used. There are exceptions to this, but I said I'd explain them when the situations arose.

After a great fish supper, we sat around the fire, drank a gallon of coffee and talked. And talked and talked and talked. Before the evening was over, I realised I was learning a lot. One thing that comes to mind is that I really believe kids have not changed much in the past few generations. They just dress funnily now; Albert, for example, wore a gold earring. When I was a kid, I'd have been laughed out of the school yard if I showed up wearing something only girls wore.

That also reminded me of another question I wanted to ask him. "Why on earth do you always wear those funny little earmuffs? It isn't even cold enough yet for electric socks."

"They're not earmuffs," he snickered. "It's my walkabout radio. Besides, it keeps the mosquitoes out of my ears."

I have to admit he had a point. I wondered why I was the only one beating myself on the head all day. I guess that's why a lot of fishermen have cauliflower ears. I considered trying the radio for a while but soon came to my senses. After all there's an unwritten dress code among outdoors men; far be it from me to break that sacred code.

While we were preparing to bunk down for the night, I took it upon myself to try to explain this code to Albert. I had just managed to get the lamp lighted, which surprised me as it hadn't worked in three years. Not wanting to seem barbaric, I removed my jacket and boots before crawling into my sleeping bag. I thought that might set a good example for the lad. I'm not sure just what happened next, but Albert explained later that I let out a wild shriek and had a look of shock and horror on my face. I remember glancing over at the boy, and yes, you guessed it, he was putting on pyjamas. Pyjamas! This younger generation must be softer than I thought.

"You can't wear them," I screamed. "It just ain't right."

As he sheepishly put them back in his duffel bag, he gave me some lame excuse about being comfortable. I told him that in order for it to be a true fishing trip comfort should not be a major consideration. "Besides," I added, "I don't need pyjamas and I'm quite cozy!" As I rolled over and drifted off to sleep, I thought to myself, "This boy is going to need a lot of intense training to become even a mediocre outdoors man."

The next morning, I rose with the vigour of a spring buck, put my hat and boots on, got a small fire started and rushed down to the lake. It was going to be a perfect day! The water was calm, a few fish were jumping, and the weather was just right. As I poured my second cup of coffee, I was startled by what sounded like an old she-bear in heat. Albert was finally getting up. I'm not quite sure what he said, but I think it was in reference to the accommodations.

"Breakfast is ready," I hollered after a few minutes of preparation.

"What? I get this treatment two days in a row?" he asked.

I knew he would appreciate the difference of camp cooking over home cooking. He asked where the nearest restaurant was. "Thanks for the offer, Albert," I said, "but I've already made your eggs. Isn't it funny how they stay clear like that instead of turning white? It must be the fresh air out here that does it."

It was kind of nice to see how Albert got along with the wildlife around us. At every meal, there always seemed to be a few seagulls hovering near where he ate. They were the strangest birds, too. They seemed to change colour before my eyes, and they flew like they were inebriated. Maybe it was some sort of mating ritual.

We were soon out on the lake and ready for action. I couldn't wait to see what this day might bring. Even Albert seemed anxious to hit the water and wet his line. The hours passed by, and the only thing that could have made this day any better would be to have caught a fish. Not even a nibble! How could this be? Albert seemed to find some humour in the situation, but I failed to see it. I had tried just about everything in my tackle box when I found it. There, in a little brown bag, in the farthest corner of the box, was the answer. My unused, untested, hom-made lure. As I opened the package, I realized it was just about the ugliest thing I had ever seen. Many years ago, I had purchased a five-cent rubber toy, stuffed a large hook through it and bragged to all my friends that some day I would catch a real lunker with it. Well, the time had come.

"Albert, this calls for drastic measures," I said. "When all else fails, go for the long shot." I explained to the lad how I had searched for the right equipment to make the supreme lure for such an occasion as today. "I searched and searched for something with just the right movement and the perfect colours. I then matched it up with just the right hook for the purpose."

Albert didn't reply. He just started searching through my tackle box. I decided right there that the kid had possibilities as a fisherman.

I was so busy working my sure-thing lure that I didn't see what Albert had put together. Somehow he had a different look about him, but I didn't pay much attention and went on with my own angling. It seemed to be within seconds that fish were coming into the boat like never before. An hour couldn't have gone by before we had a dozen nice fish. A home-made lure had finally paid off.

"Too bad your contraption didn't catch any," said Albert. "I'm sure glad you suggested we make our own. I can't remember when I've enjoyed myself as much."

Trying to remain calm, I asked, "What the heck were you using?" Before he could answer, I saw it. His earring was missing. He had attached a hook to a piece of cheap jewellery and come up with a deadly lure.

It was a quiet ride home. Albert had his funny-looking earmuffs on the whole time. I just drove and kept thinking about what had happened over the weekend. How could I ever explain to the boy it had just been a fluke?

A couple of weeks had gone by, and I decided it was time to get together again with Albert. I telephoned him and arranged to pick him up. I headed for Main Street as we chatted. I don't know what was wrong with Albert. He seemed to be almost snickering as he spoke. A couple of times he let out with a real belly laugh. I pulled into a parking space, and as we were getting out, I had just one question for the kid.

"Albert," I asked, "will it hurt much when they punch that little hole in my ear?"

Marty Roberts is a freelance writer and active member of the Outdoor Writers of Canada. He lives in Fort Erie, Ontario.

THE ROCKY SALMON HORROR SHOOT
By LaVerne Barnes

It was the photo shoot from hell. But they kept the worst part from me until it was all over.

The day started on an up note when the editor I'd been courting for three years phoned me from New York asking me to help him. The biggest-circulation hook-and-bullet magazine in North America wanted a flashy salmon shot.

His easygoing voice spelled it out. "Gotta be special. You know the kinda stuff we use. I'd like to see a 35-mm shot of someone with his rod bent double, fighting a big salmon busting out of the water. Maybe a glimpse of your great Canadian wilderness in the background. We just bought a story from a guy who's been up in your area. He wrote about the thrill of catching a big salmon. Nice piece, but we don't have any art to go with it. You probably got dozens of these pix. Can you help me?" He waited.

What a great opportunity for British Columbia to get some widespread publicity for the sports-fishing industry.

I was working on contract for one of B.C.'s tourism departments, putting together press trips, getting travel media into the province to write feature stories about the kind of stuff visiting tourists like to do. River rafting. Whale watching. Sailing. Hiking. Visiting historic sites. City nightlife. You know, the kinds of articles you see in those thick, glossy magazines near your grocery checkout or on the backs of airliner seats. The kinds of travel stories that make you salivate, pack up and go there. My strength were gardens, architecture and art.

Someone in the tourist bureau had finally figured out that a well-written, upbeat travel feature would beat the pants off advertising copy for both credibility and what they liked to call cost effectiveness. So they cut their advertising budget and went after the editorial. I was hired to get it.

Like a bunch of ageing-but-still-dimpled-cheerleader versions of Norman Vincent Peale, we wanted positive coverage, nice upbeat writing and really fabulous shots of British Columbia. The slightest criticism in anyone's column would be sent directly to the top. I always reckoned the guy at the top was laughing in his beer at all of us.

Anyway what could be more upbeat than a nice feature story about a guy coming to B.C., landing his first big salmon, and everyone reading about it in a top North American sporting magazine with a circulation of over 5 million. Pretty positive stuff. Might even bump into the fabulous zone if we could come up with a nice shot.

I kept the excitement out of my voice when I told the New York editor, "I know exactly what you need. We've got a couple of great shots we can give you to go with that story. When do you need them?"

I was lying through my teeth. I didn't know what kind of fishing shots were in our image bank. I knew we had over 5,000 slides and guessed that there would be dozens of angling images to choose from.

The editor said, "Well, we're right on deadline. This is Wednesday. I'd like to see two or three of your best by Friday afternoon. We'll pull it together on Saturday morning. I know it's real short notice. Can you do it?"

I didn't hesitate. "Absolutely. No problem. I'll look the slides over personally. Make sure you get the best. You want horizontal or vertical?"

"Doesn't matter. We'll crop as we need to. If it's a really great shot, we might give it a cover."

Jesus Murphy! A cover! I almost dropped the phone. To be on the cover of this magazine would be fantastic. The office cheerleaders would rocket into space. I allowed a small smile to creep into my voice. This New York editor wasn't going to see me all excited, howling and shrieking like some country hick. Keep it cool and jaded. They liked that. "Trust me," I said. "We won't let you down. I'll courier it myself. Give me a shout next week if you want help with the cut-line."

He hung up, contented. I charged down the hall into our image bank. "Malcolm! Toss all your fishing shots onto the light table! We've got a remarkable opportunity to get into a big cut-'n'-gut book, but we don't have much time."

Malcolm looked at me blankly. "What fishing shots? The stuff we had was so old and tired we pitched it all last year. No budget to buy anything new."

So here it was. Wednesday morning. Those promised pictures had to be in New York by Friday afternoon. And the cupboard was bare. God was getting me for something.

Wait a minute! What about Frank, the photographer on Vancouver Island who'd been begging me to use him for fishing shots? Perfect. He could get that hot new guide up in Campbell River to pull a big salmon out of the water near Haig-Browne's old area. I got him on his cellular phone.

"Jesus, Barnes, you just don't go out and hook into a bloody great honking tyee like snapping your fingers. I mean, are you nuts, or what? You sure as hell don't know anything about fishing."

"Listen to me, Frank. Think about this magazine. All the outdoor types read it. I've promised the editor a great action shot of someone catching a big chinook. Something impressive. Dramatic. By Friday. Think of the promotional value for B.C. Think of your name on the photo credit. Think how much you're going to get paid for this shot."

He thought. "Okay. Maybe we'll get lucky. The guide's name is Craig. He's a friend. There's an old secret hole I've never told anyone about. A 10-year-old kid pulled out a 37 pound fish near the area last week. I'll get Craig, and we'll call you later from the river if we have any luck. But the weather's against us. It's too hot."

"It's summer, remember? The days are long, Frank. My dad used to swear that last light was best for bringing up fish. I can just see that shot you're going to give us. Backlit, the deep water blackened by the gloom of those big evergreens hanging out over the bank, an explosion of silver spray, the massive body of a perfect salmon fighting for his life, the setting sun outlining the bent rod and sweating face of a guy up to his belly in the water, his dark-green chest waders gleaming. Yeah!"

He paused. "God, Barnes. Your dad was a fly-fisherman. He went after brook trout. He never caught a salmon in his life."

"Yes, well, whatever. A fish is still a fish, eh? You guys have got to come up with something. I'm working late tonight. Stay in touch with me."

The remainder of the day went into the bucket. I kept working, but I was nervous as an old bride having second thoughts about everything including life. Why did I promise something before checking first? It would have taken about 30 seconds to learn we had no fishing shots. If I promised something and couldn't deliver, my credibility with this editor would be a joke. I wondered whether it would help if I threw up for an hour. The day dragged by. It was hard to concentrate on anything.

I was packing up when the phone rang. It was Frank on his cellular. I glanced out the window. Just on dusk. Last light. My dad had been right.

"Holy Mother of God!" Frank was laughing and choking all at once. "Craig has hooked a steelhead. It's the biggest goddam steelhead I've ever seen. Must be 35 pounds, easy. He almost lost it, but he's still got it on the line. He's down there now, kind of kneeling in the water with the fish chomping at the hook glaring up at him. Put up one hell of a fight. I've got some unbelievable shots!"

I remember saying, "Frank, get off the phone and tell Craig to throw it back. I don't want a steelhead shot. The story is about a chinook. And 35 pounds isn't big enough!"

His voice cracked my eardrums. "A 35 pound steelhead isn't big enough? This is the biggest steelhead we've seen on this river in 20 years! Of course we'll release the fish. That's the law. Craig just thought you might want a shot of him easing it back into the deep water. Listen, we're not going to get anything better than this."

I felt like I was standing on his head. "Look, Frank, it's probably a great shot of a beautiful fish. But it's not what the editor asked me for. It won't go with the story. I deal with these guys all the time. They're bloody single-minded once they've set their course."

I was hoping he wouldn't break down and cry.

"Frank, do this. You and Craig say goodbye to the fish. Go get cleaned up. Have a couple of beers. On me. Tomorrow morning at dawn, give it another go. If you don't get anything big by noon, I'll call New York and talk to the editor."

He hung up on me.

The next morning I was in early, but there were no messages. I was surprised when Frank called two hours before lunch. His voice was strangely calm and held a peculiar edge. "You got your shot."

He waited.

"That 35 pound steelhead come back for another scar on his lip?"

"No." He was choking back a snort. "It's a chinook. Almost 50 pounds. Craig used his custom-built graphite rod. We didn't fool around with light tackle. A couple of perfect dawn shots. Nice fish. Got several fine pictures of the fish coming right up out of the water just like you ordered. My package is on the Vancouver float plane. You should have it within the hour. Lots of time to courier them on to New York."

This wasn't like Frank. Something weird was happening. A 50 pound chinook made most grown men shout. What was going on here? It almost sounded like he was trying not to laugh.

"Frank? You okay? This is amazing news. Honestly, I can hardly believe it. I mean, two big fish on the same river in less than 24 hours. Maybe I should call the Campbell River TV newsroom and line you guys up for an interview. What did you do with the fish?"

He laughed uneasily. "Naw. Don't bother. I'm okay. We're both a little hung-over from all those beers we got rid of last night after we released the steelhead. We were up before dawn, back on the river. Craig is bushed. I'm bagged too. We're going up to Port McNeil for a few days. I'll call you next week."

"Where's the fish now?" I could have sworn I heard someone laughing.

"Craig gave it to his mother. It's already in the oven. I think a couple of curling teams are coming over for dinner. See you next week."

The line went dead.

Good as his word, his package showed up before noon. There were half a dozen superb shots of a scene almost identical to the one I had described to him the day before. An angler, backlit, his dark-green chest waders gleaming in the early morning light, stood in a pool darkened by the shadow of big evergreen trees looming in the background, his rod bent almost double, a massive silver chinook exploding out of a tsunami 30 feet away. Breathtaking!

There was no way a shot like this could be faked.

Within minutes the precious slides were in a courier package to New York. I knew the editor would be delighted.

When the magazine came out three months later, I was sitting at my desk admiring Frank's great shots when he walked in. I hadn't talked to him since the shoot.

"Congratulations, Frank," I smiled. "They used three of your shots. Did you see your photo credit right under the writer's byline? Great work. I wish we could have paid you more for this shoot. Pity they didn't use one of your shots on the cover. But it's great publicity. Everyone's excited."

He closed my door, sat down and grinned.

"Okay, Barnes. I've forgiven you for not wanting my steelhead picture. The magazine is on the stands now, so I'll tell you what really happened."

"The way I remember it, Frank, you guys set some kind of record. Caught two amazing fish in less than 24 hours."

Frank laughed. "Amazing, yes. Caught? Not exactly.

"Craig and I both knew the chances of us getting a big salmon the next day were microscopic. Both of us were pissed off at you for not wanting our steelhead photo. After we had a few beers that night, Craig told me about his cousin who owns a commercial fish boat. The idea just kind of planted itself. The boat was due in at midnight, so we walked down to the docks, found the boat and explained our problem.

"We had a few more brewskis, and Craig's cousin helped us pick out a big, fresh chinook. Must have been close to 50 pounds. God, just a gorgeous brute. No net marks. All the scales intact. Eyes shining as bright as Jack Nicholson's.

"Yes, it was gutted out. We put it on ice, wrapped it in plastic and carried it as tenderly as a newborn babe to the back seat of my Volvo. We went back to the river, had a few more beers and waited for the sun to come up.

"Craig got out his custom-built graphite rod and tied the line right into the bottom jaw of the salmon. I think he used 40, maybe even 50 pound test.

"I positioned Craig where the sun would catch him from behind and set up a remote-control strobe to play some extra light off the fish. He waded out into the water and simply threw the salmon into the river, let it float downstream and began jerking it up out of the water. Like he was fighting and landing it. You know."

He began to laugh. I thought I was going to pass out.

"It didn't work. The gutted pink flaps of the salmon's belly kept turning toward the camera. I went through two rolls of 36 on my motor drive.

"By this time we were both laughing so hard we had to have another beer. Then Craig solved the problem. It was a weight and balance thing, he said. The fish needed more weight in his gut. Well, what used to be his gut.

"So we carried the fish up on the bank, laid it carefully on a plastic bag so it wouldn't lose any scales, and stuffed it full of stones. Those nice, smooth river rocks about three inches across. We had to hurry because we wanted a backlit shot, remember? Dawn was just breaking. Craig used some light leader to stitch up the flaps, kind of overlapping it so the rocks wouldn't pop out.

"We had a helluva time carrying the damned thing back to the river. The current was dragging at Craig. A 50 pound chinook is a beast to carry. And we were both laughing so hard we couldn't see.

"On his first few throws, I thought I might lose them both. And then the damned fish kept wanting to turn his belly at us to show off his stitches. Kind of a Boris Karloff version of Frankenstein's tyee. But after a few practice runs we got it right.

"Craig was out there hurling the fish filled with rocks, cursing and grunting and whacking the salmon up out of the river like something out of *Jurassic Park*, screaming, 'My arms! My arms!' And we were both hysterical, damned near wetting ourselves. Howling at everything. Even when the tip of Craig's custom rod broke, even then. It was all too much.

"The shots were great, eh?" His whole body began shaking as he started laughing again.

I'd gone beyond shock. Beyond rage. As hard as I tried not to, I was bent over laughing. But I had to have the last word. "Frank," I said, "you deserve your cheque. Pity you didn't make the cover, though."

"Take another look, Barnes," he smiled.

A young man was kneeling in a fast-moving stream, cradling a beautiful big rainbow-coloured fish gleaming wet in the light. The camera looked down onto his handsome face filled with tenderness and pure joy. It was Frank's shot of the young guide, Craig, just before he released the 35 pound steelhead back into the wild river.

LaVerne Barnes is Manager, Media Relations for the Tourism Market Development Branch in the Ministry of Small Business, Tourism and Culture in British Columbia and author of *The Plastic Orgasm* and *Fish Me a Clean Fish.* She lives in Vancouver, British Columbia.

THEY REALLY FIGHT HARD HERE
By Geoff Coleman

One thing that anglers from different parts of Canada will defend to the death is the superior fighting ability of fish from their neck of the woods. Some claim New Brunswick's smallmouth are tougher to boat than any bass in Quebec and that Atlantic salmon are easier to catch than chinooks and so on. I have witnessed three of the most impressive fights ever, and all were in Ontario muskellunge waters.

The first was on a lake where I was fishing for wall-eye. We were dropping those slow trolls into a light breeze along a shoreline, when in the distance we could see another guy in a car topper making quite a commotion while trying to land a fish. When we got within shouting distance, he informed us he had hooked this monster about 20 minutes earlier, and that each time he got it close to the boat, it would take off on another strong run.

He was equipped with heavy line and a stout rod, and we figured that within a few minutes he'd be able to boat the trophy, so we cut the engine and watched the show. He told us how he had come out to this spot and anchored, hoping to catch some wall-eye. He cast out a jig and minnow and was hopping it back to the boat when the fish slammed it. He was able to slowly gain line on the fish until it was almost under the boat, and then the hog would steam off in another direction.

After seeing this process three or four times, one of the guys in my boat suggested we shove off and give the lucky fisherman some room to fight it out, free of distractions. It seemed like a strange suggestion, considering we might be able to see a huge fish come up at any moment, but Joe insisted we continue on our way.

When we were out of earshot, Joe could contain himself no longer and burst out laughing. He had twigged to what was really going on in the epic battle down the shore.

The guy was snagged on bottom, and because he had left a fair bit of slack in the anchor rope when he tied it off, he was actually able to winch the boat back to the snag with the heavy mono he was using. At some point, as he was towing the boat to the snag, the wind would pick up and blow the boat downwind to the end of the anchor rope, making the angler believe it was the fish that was moving. At the end of the "run"–when the wind died down–he would recover line and again pull the boat towards the snag.

We watched this for a while, trying desperately not to sound like a pack of hyenas each time the guy said something about the fish taking off for the 14th time. We continued fishing. The fun came in seeing how long the guy would try to fight it out with his trophy. We're not sure how long that took because it got too dark to see. He had lots of help though. At least four boats were standing by waiting to see this giant come to the net.

The second fight was on Sturgeon Lake near Fenelon Falls in the Kawarthas. Steve was fishing for anything that would come by on a gorgeous summer day. He tossed out his hook and minnow and settled back to enjoy the sunshine and scenery. As he watched a loon fishing in the shadows near shore, he felt a tug on his line and set the hooks. The fish had some weight to it so he guessed a nice bass had hit, but when it waged a deep battle, he decided a three or four pound wall-eye must be on the line. A few minutes later when he had not been able to raise it from bottom, he realized that he too must have hooked a muskellunge.

Exerting all the pressure he dared on the six-pound-test line, he worked the beast toward the boat. In the stained Sturgeon Lake water he couldn't see the fish except for a thick, black shadow that raced furiously beneath the boat. It tired and started to play dead, giving Steve his chance to pull the fish toward a waiting landing net that was starting to look ridiculously small.

He lifted the rod, and the fish followed lazily until it saw the boat and made its first jump. It might have been the black body with white spots that alerted Steve to the fact that he had not hooked a muskie, or it might have been that the fish had abnormally large fins. Whatever the case, after the jump, Steve quickly realized he had hooked the partner of the loon he had seen earlier. Now he had to contend with an angry, 25 pound bird that could make the crows in Hitchcock's *The Birds* look like Big Bird from *Sesame Street*, while an equally enraged male loon loudly and threateningly circled closer and closer.

Fortunately the line broke before Steve had to switch from fighting a fish to wrestling a loon, thus avoiding his first brush with the exciting world of veterinary surgery.

The final battle was with a friend Bob who had access to a lake that had what he humbly called "the hardest-fighting 'lunge you'll ever catch. They may not be huge, but they'll fight like they're twice their size." We had to use the biggest crank baits we could find, and they had to be painted with a muskie pattern. Evidently cannibalism produces the toughest fighters.

Few lures met the rigorous standard that Bob demanded in terms of paint job, so he normally took a finished bait to an artist friend and had him make it as lifelike as possible. The result was a remarkably accurate representation of a muskie that was hard to tell from the real thing.

So off we went on the third Sunday in June, trolling our custom-painted minnow baits. Within an hour, Bob hooked a monster muskie that actually straightened out the snap on the wire leader he was using. We watched as she finned slowly out of sight, the metallic green crank bait trailing from the outside of her cheek where the tail hook was impaled from her sideways attack.

We continued fishing after that, though Bob lacked his earlier enthusiasm. I'm not sure if he was more upset over losing the fish or losing a piece from the closest thing he has to an art collection. With spirits flagging, we decided to try for some wall-eye and tied on cheap, lead-head jigs, nothing more than decorator prints.

On the first cast, Bob was fast to a fish, and after 10 seconds, it was obvious it was another muskie. It stayed down, tearing around the rocks like a world-record-holding sprinter being chased by a Pit Bull until Bob actually asked me to pour water on his reel because it was overheating. I asked if he would like a rod rest and fighting chair as well, but he just muttered something about turning the boat around to chase his fish and "I hope it doesn't try to ram us."

As the battle continued, it became clear this was a very substantial fish. After another few minutes of bottom hugging, the fish suddenly gave up and was pulled easily, like dead weight, towards the surface. As it came closer, I stood poised with a landing net and braced for the explosion that would follow the game of possum.

But there was no explosion. All that came up was a jig and a hand-painted muskie bait. Bob had hooked the lure that was still stuck in the cheek of the 'lunge he had lost earlier. During all the thrashing of the fight, with Bob pulling one way and the muskie the other, the magnum Rapala was eventually yanked out of the fish. That was the point where the muskie suddenly "gave up."

And now there it was, three feet below us, the jig hook caught right in the tie ring of the same hand-painted muskie bait Bob had lost earlier. As Bob reeled it in the last few feet, it looked for all the world like a seven-inch muskie had hit the jig and was about to be netted.

I turned to Bob and cracked, "You were right; they really do fight hard in this lake."

Geoff Coleman is one of Ontario's top outdoor writers with credits in every major fishing magazine. When not fishing, writing or taking pictures, he is a high-school geography teacher in Fenelon Falls, Ontario.

SPLITTING HAIRS
By Marty Roberts

The April meeting of the Shoot and Hook Outdoors Society was about to begin, and naturally I was very excited. I had been to a couple of meetings already, but this was the first time that I had been invited. Ol' Doc Williams had called my house earlier in the day to say that he was very tied up with "doctorin' stuff" and wouldn't have time to pick up "necessities fer the meetin'."

This meant that I would be responsible for preparing something to eat for myself and the six members of the club, as well as beverages. I knew it would be fruitless to ask my mother to help, mainly because she didn't approve of me socializing with what she called "those old reprobates." I did the next best thing. I went straight to Granny's house. She wasn't your normal grandmother. She was a great believer that a boy wasn't a boy unless he was up to some sort of mischief. She began the luncheon preparations right away.

I was the first to show up at Doc Williams' for the meeting, only to find him catching 40 winks on his makeshift operating table in the clinic. Doc told me to put the sandwiches out in the back room because it was cooler there. He also said I shouldn't have brought the soda pop "'cause that stuff'll rot yer pipes."

I opened the door to the back room and was hit with a waft of alcohol mixed with very cold air. I reached along the wall for the light switch but couldn't find it right away. I set the basket of sandwiches down on a table that I felt beside me and then found the switch. Turning to pick up the basket, I let out a scream and was later fined 10 ¢ for the words that issued so easily from what I was told was a foul mouth.

I had set the basket on a table all right. Also occupying that table was the old widow McDougall. I was sure it was her because the only thing visible from under the white sheet was the shiniest silver-blue hair I had ever seen.

"Doc," I asked, "what's Mrs. McDougall doing in the back room?"

"Well," he said, "I'm waitin' fer the undertaker to pick her up. That room's 'bout the coolest I got, and besides I can't stand the stench of that perfume she always has on."

Before long my nerves had got somewhat back to normal, and the meeting was well under way. Uncle Thornald and Cousin Jimmy were still chuckling at my experience, and Hal and Ernie just looked plain disgusted with me. They had never felt this "kid" belonged at the Shoot and Hook Outdoor Society meetings. Pastor Buck McElroy at least had the decency to go in and say a quick prayer over the dear old lady, he emerged soon after with a couple of sandwiches in hand.

The whole purpose of the meeting was first to discuss where everyone would like to go for opening day of trout season the following week, and next, to tie a few flies in preparation for the trip. Although fly tying was not new to me, I was a little nervous. After all, here I was with the most renowned fishermen in town and trying to come up with a fly that would actually catch a fish. That would be a first in my books.

I glanced over every now and then to see the others busy at the job at hand. I, however, was at a standstill. I had all the makings for a decent fly but soon discovered the members of the society were prone to invent their own flies, complete with original name. What I needed was some material for a really good hackle. I took a break to fetch the sandwiches for the boys.

I was soon back at the table, tying furiously to catch up to the others. In fact, I was able to complete three very nice flies that evening and was sure to be ready for those brookies on Saturday morning.

It turned out better than I could ever have expected. Each member of the society took their place on Catfish Creek. I, of course, was sent down to the furthest reaches of the creek. Within minutes I had landed two nice trout, whereupon Pastor Buck promptly kicked me out so he could take over "his" spot.

This sort of displacement went on all morning, but no matter where I went, my luck followed. At lunch time, I had my limit while the others were still trying to catch their first. Finally Doc asked me what kind of fly I was using.

"It's the one I tied the other night," I replied, handing the deadly piece of tackle over to him.

"Boy, thet's the queerest dang fly I ever done seen," said Uncle Thornald. "But thet purty silvery-blue colour sure does seem to fool the brookies. Whatcha name thet thing?"

"Well," I answered sheepishly, "in honour of the donor of the hackle, I think I'll call it the Widow McDougall Wisp."

Marty Roberts is a freelance writer and active member of the Outdoor Writers of Canada. He lives in Fort Erie, Ontario.

TYEE
By David Carpenter

You may not be aware of this, but all across North America there is a club for sexually disabled fishermen–Sexually Disabled Anglers International (SDAI). When you join up, the High Archon introduces you, and you offer testimony to the fellows in the clubhouse. I haven't been a member for very long, but already I can see that we all tell just about the same story. It usually starts something like this:

"Speak, Brother," the Archon says.

"My name is Bob Loblaw, and I have a problem. It all started when I took the wife out for a quick troll before dark. I hadn't caught a fish in three days an' she ties into this big pike, hauls 'er in . . ."

And here's the moment we all start to nod in recognition.

" . . . and this lunker she brought in, it weighed 29 pounds. Bigger'n any pike I ever seen, let alone hauled in myself."

There will be murmurs of sadness from the anglers in the room. Moans of consolation. And then the sad confession:

"Ever since that night, well, . . . me an' the wife . . ."

"Say it, Brother," cries the Archon.

"Well, let's put it this way," the poor man might conclude. "You can't shoot pool with a rope."

My name is David Carpenter, and I have a problem. After my testimony at the SDAI an old fellow came up to me and asked me to elaborate.

"It was a rainbow trout," I told him. "Seven pounds, 12 ounces. Huge. She took it on a fly. I offered to bring it in for her, and she gave me this . . ."

The old fellow shot me a look of recognition. "Withering look?"

"That's it! A withering look!"

"Why not go out an' catch one bigger? Up north the lake trout go 15-20 pounds reg'lar."

I shook my head. "My wife, she's a purist. I brainwashed her. It's got to be something real jumpy, sporty. And it's gotta be light tackle."

"Then why don't you go for a tyee? That'd do the trick."

"A tyee?"

I've never believed in guardian angels; I don't even believe in good luck. I'm from Saskatchewan. So imagine my surprise when, shortly after the above conversation at the SDAI clubhouse, the phone rang. It was Jim Sutherland of *Western Living:* "How would you like to catch the biggest salmon you have ever seen? I need a writer/angler."

"You mean . . . catch a? . . ."

"That's right," he said. "A tyee."

Tyee is the Salish word for "chief." When a spring salmon (sometimes called chinook) gets to be 30 pounds or better, it becomes a tyee. In British Columbia an entire corporation has been built on this big fish, and its most illustrious fishing camp is Painter's Lodge in Campbell River. This lodge is a mile or so from the Tyee Club, the spiritual home of the most venerable salmon derby in Canada. For almost a century, VIP anglers from all over the world have been coming to Painter's Lodge, a sort of Taj Mahal of fishing camps. Their desire is to catch a tyee and then join the club. The King of Siam, Glen Ford, Zane Grey, Bob Hope, all have come here around the end of August to distinguish themselves in that utterly primitive fashion – killing a mighty salmon.

One of the keenest anglers is the manager of fishing operations at Painter's Lodge, Wayne Dreger. He speaks with the nervous energy of a dynamite blaster, and when he describes the technique of striking a tyee, his entire body seems to tense up like Boris Becker before a serve.

"You watch that rod tip," he says. "You don't take your eyes off it. You may want to talk to your buddy, but that doesn't mean you can take your eyes off your tip. Remember this is not fun. It is utter concentration. The very second your tip flutters, you strike as though your life depended on it."

My buddy for this trip is an old friend and photographer from Vancouver, Pete Nash. Already he has located our guide and rower, a young man named Randy. He tells us to be ready the next morning by 5:15. Nash doesn't know that I am here for another more urgent reason.

A wake-up call at 4 a.m. Nash and I drift outside in a west-coast wooze of fetal memories. Randy is out on the wharf. We are going fishing. As they say out here, we are going to row a tyee.

The Tyee Club rules state that fishermen must not use a motor while fishing. Our rowboat has a motor, but we can only use it to get out to the tyee pool. Nash mans the motor while our guide, Randy gets the tackle ready. We are using seven foot rods with single-action reels, 20-pound-test line and large Gibbs-Stewart spoons. Randy is forever shining these spoons as though they were pieces from the royal family's tea service. Randy is obviously the right man for this job. In many ways an ordinary guy, in matters of angling, he is a perfectionist.

We skim over the chuck, and the night begins to lift out of the estuary. Shapes loom out of the dark: islands, rocks, hills. We have entered an outdoor gallery of Toni Onley sketches that drift out of the twilight in a dream of yammering gulls. Randy waves a hand at Nash to cut the engine.

My rod tip bobs up and down with the dodging rhythm of the spoon. I hold my thumb on the spool of my single-action reel. When the rod tip flutters, I will not feel the strike. But I will strike back nonetheless. I will yank that thing back so hard I will almost break the rod or my back. Nash is thinking the same thoughts, I am sure. Grim. We are a disciplined duo, and we are not–no, absolutely not–having fun. Neither the gentle weather nor Randy's unfailing good humour will alter our Prussian demeanour.

"Nash, having fun?"

"Nope."

"Good."

"How about you, Carp? Having fun?"

"Nope."

"Good."

Our first shift ends around 8:30. Just as we are turning to go for breakfast, Randy looks up from polishing my spoon. "Dave," he says, "did you feel anything out there this morning? Even a nudge?"

"Not a thing. Why?"

"There's a tooth mark on your spoon."

In five days, about 500 keeners rowed the tyee pool. Not one tyee was killed. We saw them though, rolling out of the ocean like economy sized orcas or slapping the surface with their tails. They were there, huge and beautiful, too huge to imagine laying comfortably in our small boat. Too beautiful to imagine dead, a mere trophy emblematic of some guy's manhood. Even *my* manhood, which I had almost forgotten about. Seeing the big salmon roll made me wonder. Like the keenest anglers in the Tyee Club, I am trying to kill this creature I admire so much–not by purchasing a tin of salmon in the K-mart or any other act of consumer boredom–but by fooling it with my patience and my art. Killing a mighty fish is not a moral act; it is a primitive act. Don't be fooled by the cane rods and the tweed coats worn by the old anglers of the Tyee Club. Yes, they are gentlemen, but when they take or harvest or beard or finesse a salmon, the verb they use is kill. Killing a mighty salmon takes us back, however briefly, to our most primitive origins when fishing well meant eating well. The man or woman beholds the creature helpless and flopping in the boat, beholds how fat and deep the body, how silver the sides, how perfectly streamlined for long runs and mighty leaps. It may be the first angler at the dawn of time who looks at the fish and says, "Tyee."

Well, Nash and I were skunked. Randy offered us a frozen salmon, but (having, I suppose, our pride) we turned him down.

My adventure has a postscript. Alone in my car on the last leg of my journey back to Saskatoon, I had a strong urge to throw out the old fly line. I did a little detour to a lake known for its bruiser rainbows. I had no boat, but I knew of a spot where you can fly cast from shore without your back cast getting fouled. It was a beautiful day, but this time there wasn't a person in sight. Why is it that these moments come invariably when your photographer buddy and all witnesses are miles away?

Well, I guess you know what happened. On the first cast from shore, my fly landed about 35 feet in front of me. I waited while it bobbed on the surface, then pulled it under and began to jerk the big fly toward shore. There was a monumental surge where my fly had been, and I saw a dark back and the flash of a big dorsal. My reel was buzzing, and my fly was being carried at violent speed toward the centre of the lake. When I checked the first long run, the rainbow swam right for me, and I had to strip in line as fast as I could. Then the fish wheeled and did a slow leap out into the blue, terrific sky. It seemed to hang there in defiance of gravity and re-enter as softly as an otter sliding into a pool. I think it fair to say that this, too, was Tyee in another of his magnificent guises. The Chief had come to call.

It took about 15 minutes to tire the fish and about five more to head it into a shallow channel where the canoes are launched. Two feet long, as deep bodied as its Pacific cousins, and built for power rushes and acrobatics. A 10-pound rainbow trout. These are about as common as large emeralds in your back garden. It might come as no surprise to my readers that I released this fish without hesitation. Who was I, after all, to presume to spill the blood of the Chief? Unhooked, the fish lay stunned and exhausted in the channel, righted itself, and with a shudder from its powerful tail, ploughed away from the shallow water, leaving behind an impressive wake.

I had a very pleasant drive across the prairie all the way to Saskatoon. I had only one lingering doubt. When I walk into the kitchen with an empty cooler and tell my wife, Honor, that I just released the biggest rainbow either of us has ever seen, will she believe me?

I love those forlorn fishermen at the old SDAI clubhouse.

How I shall miss them!

David Carpenter is a Saskatoon, Saskatchewan, writer. His works of fiction include *God's Bedfellows* and *Jokes for the Apocalypse*. His latest book is *Fishing in the West*.

MUSKIE'S DAY OUT
By Ray Dillon

Muskie Bainbridge was a fisherman. There was no doubt about that. He lived and breathed fishing, he ate and drank fishing, and he dreamed fishing. On his wedding day, he rushed to the altar wearing a tuxedo and waders, apologizing to an irate bride who swore she'd change him or kill him and it didn't much matter which. On the day when the first of seven children arrived, Muskie was fishing, but he did arrive at the hospital in time to see Mommy offer the first night feeding, some 10 hours later.

Muskie had difficulty holding down a job. It seemed that when fishing season came, Muskie became overwhelmed by sickness: colds, headaches and flu. It was fate that brought his boss out onto the river one morning in June when Muskie was supposed to be sick in bed. "That you over in that boat, Muskie?" he called out.

"Ah, no boss, it's one of the other guys," Muskie replied. "They kidnapped me and forced me to come out here, sick as I am." Muskie didn't have a large brain despite eating lots of fish, and after June 3, that fateful morning, he had one less job.

Muskie wasn't his real name. Adolphus Herman Eldridge Bainbridge was born on the first day of April 1951 in a small cabin in the Blue Ridge Mountains of Tennessee. He grew up in the backwoods, fishing and hunting, barefoot most of the time and bathing only when he got caught out in the rain. Hence, he acquired the nickname Muskie, not from the famous fish that proliferate up north, but from his body odour acquired down south, and it stuck.

Muskie was middle-aged now, with a sagging beer belly, a scruffy unshaven face, round shoulders and big, long, hairy arms. Actually when I met him, I began to believe in Darwin's theory of evolution 'cause Muskie looked like he was half man, half anthropoid, or maybe it was 70:30, with the 30 per cent being man. A sloping forehead and two beady eyes set deep in a permanent scowl, Muskie was not your picture of grace and beauty. He always wore the same pair of dirty, old blue jeans held up with a pair of moth-eaten bright red braces. The rear of his jeans hung low, giving all a peek at the big crevice. An old pair of floppy sneakers that literally smoked when he'd walk or amble, set off this Bubba, I'm Yours image.

Muskie always walked throughout the community seeing as how he couldn't drive a vehicle. He had attempted to get a driver's licence once but not being educated and being such a slow lad, after several wrecks, he gave up, as did the townspeople who tried to teach him. Thus, Muskie was doomed to a life of low-paying labour jobs and fishing in the local hot spots. Muskie's bride, a heavily freckled, buck-toothed wisp of a lass, had been in a rush to get to the altar and probably wasn't too particular with whom. After all she was 14 years old at the time, practically an old maid in her mountain-country homeland. They seemed suited for each other.

Muskie had been having some financial difficulty with a boat purchase, and after losing yet another job in early June, the sheriff's department was nosing around looking for that car-topper with the 9.9 Merc' outboard. One morning in late June, Muskie was doing some sin circles in Guv'ner Lake. A sin circle, as Muskie would explain it, was several large circles done at high speed by a fisherman either too hung-over to realise it or too drunk to care.

"It kinda herds the fish into one spot," his three-toothed grin would slur. "Then you sit down and shut that engine off and wait 'til everything quiets down. After that, if you're still awake, you bait up and chuck 'er over the side and right into the middle of them herded up fish and bang! If they're bass you got in that circle, they'll come a tail walkin' right to the boat. If they're trout, then they'll run deep and keep on circlin' 'til they're plumb tuckered. Then they'll come to the surface, on their sides, paddlin' round and round with one fin. That'll kill 'em 'cause God meant for fish to swim on their bellies, not their sides."

So much for the Reverend Bainbridge and his fishin' rodeo. Gettin' back to the sin circles and Muskie's flight from the long arm of the law, Muskie saw that sheriff come a stumblin' down over the embankment and splashin' out into the cold lake water.

"Muskie Bainbridge? I'm Sheriff Pinworm from the county. I'm here by virtue . . . " and Muskie revved the outboard.

"I can't hear ya," Muskie yelled back.

The sheriff cleared his throat. "I'm here to . . . " The engine revved again, and Muskie circled in close. "Bring that damned boat here now!" Muskie sped off into an even larger circle.

It probably would have ended in a stalemate with the sheriff yelling and Muskie continuing to circle about had it not been for fate. Muskie's line was trailing the craft, bouncing and spinning in the motor's wake when the big pickerel hit the lure. The reel screamed and started emptying line. Muskie forgot about the sheriff and concentrated on grabbing his pole. The boat motor straightened out and sent the car topper rushing for the rocks and shore, several yards from the frustrated sheriff. Muskie, not realizing the gravity of the situation, reeled in the pickerel and held it aloft. "I got 'em, Pinworm! I got 'em! Ain't he a beaut? Oh, shit-t-t-t-!"

The aftermath was a foregone conclusion. Pinworm got what was left of the boat after the rocks redesigned the hull and sides. Muskie was thrown clear and lay in the mud and debris on the shoreline, still clutching the writhing pickerel. The sheriff would have charged Muskie, but since Muskie was already on the county charity line, there would be no point. "Half of nuthin' is nuthin'," old Muskie would say. The sheriff took the twisted, gouged boat with him, and Muskie sloped off home with supper.

That was the first of many encounters with Sheriff Pinworm, and perhaps I'd better clarify the name. The pronunciation of the sheriff's name is Pinor, with the "w" and "m" left silent. He was a misplaced Scandinavian of sorts with some German and French thrown in, and I believe he was illegitimate since everyone I knew called him a bastard.

Muskie took special pride in aggravating the sheriff. He'd get obnoxiously drunk, Muskie that is, and go into the little town's jail overnight to sleep it off. Of course the sheriff had to oblige him since the laws of the land wouldn't let vagrants or inebriated citizens wander about unattended. Muskie knew that much, although he'd never been formally educated. Muskie did go through school, something he was quite proud of and would occasionally tell prospective employers when he felt like work, once every three or four years. "I . . . ah . . . went through school, ya know. Yep! One morning, my daddy sent me over with a load of wood for the stove. I wandered clean through 'er lookin' for a teacher. Course she wasn't there!"

When the fishin' fever hit, Muskie would slap his missus on her bony rump, grab his favourite fishin' pole and say to hell with all the bills. He claimed to have a nervous disposition and the stress of everyday work just wouldn't allow him to continue any job. One particular morning in early July, Muskie decided to have a day off. We never did figure what he was taking the day off from, but it would prove to be a memorable day out for Muskie Bainbridge.

Since Muskie didn't drive, he'd often sling his old knapsack over his shoulder, pick up his creel and pole and strike off down the dusty back roads, heading for one of the lakes beyond the small mountain town. This morning he had decided to go to Ghost Lake, a crystal-clear body of water tucked neatly between two lazy mountain-sized hills. The lake had some of the best trout fishing to be had in the Blue Ridge mountains, and although the ivy covered most of the trees in the area giving the entire landscape a creepy effect, Muskie didn't mind. He didn't believe in ghosts.

As the middle-aged vagrant ambled through town, the local dogs came visitin'. They'd growl and snap at him, encouraged by some of the teen hooligans who'd follow along teasing Muskie. "Them dogs gonna eat ya, Muskie," one red-haired, freckle-faced kid taunted.

"Not if I eat them first," Muskie grinned and switched his fishin' pole.

The red-headed kid ran up on the old porch to his grandpa. "Grandpa, ain't old Muskie a sight?" The wrinkled tobacco-juice grin was Grandpa's only reply.

"Good day, Mr. Peabody," Muskie rasped. "Funny how a red-headed kid is put together, ain't it? Either he's so damned good lookin' that the stars'll fall from the sky, . . . 'er he's so homely, ugly and scroungy that only the dogs'll listen to him. Must be God's revenge on cousins inbreeding," he laughed and walked on.

The kids watched him go, shuffling down the main drag in a cloud of dust. It wasn't long until Muskie was approaching the trail that wound through the hills to Ghost Lake. "H-m-m-m-m-m! I ain't afraid! I ain't afraid!" Muskie spoke loudly to reassure himself that the fishing would be fine and no spooks would come near him. He sipped loudly on a can of cold beer and tossed the empty into the bushes as he stumbled along. Muskie never was too concerned about the environment. He had attended one conference on the holes in the ozone layer, mistaking the ozone holes for some new place to fish. When the first speaker had pounded a fist on the podium and stated that we must all cut back on using spray cans of deodorant and hair spray and perfume, Muskie got up and shouted, "I've been doin' my part, your worship," and left amidst tumultuous laughter.

As Muskie continued to the lake, he drank several more beers, figuring that the more he drank, the lighter his load would be. By the time he got to the lake, his load was much lighter, and so was his head.

Unbeknown to Muskie, a pair of young lovers shared the cool shade of some big oak trees overlooking the lake's outlet. So enamoured with each other were they that they never heard the belches and huffing and puffing of the fisherman as he plunked down on the shoreline to cast his baited line.

Muskie hooked into a fat trout on his first cast, but even after he had landed it and sipped another cold beer, he was starting to have second thoughts about Ghost Lake. He could hear the occasional moan coming from the surrounding woods, and to his knowledge, nobody ever came out here. "Nah-h-h-h! There ain't no such thing as a ghost," he reassured himself. He took a big slurp of beer, allowing it to run down his three-day growth of beard onto a hairy chest and belly. It felt cool, but what was this?

"A-h-h-h-h. O-h-h-h-h-h! U-h-h-h-h-h-h!"

The noise was getting louder, and it sounded like there was some heavy breathing goin' on. The hair was rising on the back of Muskie's sweaty neck. "Who's there?" he queried. The bushes thrashed and more moans came forth. "I said who's there?" Muskie gulped down something hard that seemed to stick in his throat. It was fear and no cold beer would wash that down.

"O-h-h-h-h-h! A-h-h-h-h-h! N-o-o-o-o-o! O-o-o-o-o-o-o-o, yes!"

The trail never seemed so short nor his pack so light as Muskie bounced his bulk up through the woods and headed homeward, darting fearful glances back over his shoulder. He tripped a couple of times and hurt his pride but other than that, made good time. As he quick marched through town, he paused at the old garage that offered cold soda, cold beer and gasoline. The old, grease-smeared proprietor rocked back and forth in the afternoon heat, shaded by a sagging porch. He hailed Muskie.

"How'd ya make out, Muskie? Get any fish?"

"Got one, Ezra, but the dangdest thing happened to me out to Ghost Lake. Ya ever heard a ghost?"

"No. Cain't say's I have," came the old mechanic's reply.

"Well," Muskie rolled his eyes towards what little grey matter he might have had for a brain, "I heard one. It was a moanin' and a groanin'! It was awful! Every time I'd cast my fishin' line into that lake, it would moan, 'Take it out! O-o-o-o-o! Take it out.' And every time I'd reel in and get ready to go, it'd moan 'O-o-o-o-o-o! Put it back in! Put it back in!' I got so danged confused, I hightailed it outta there."

As Muskie shared his hauntin' with Ezra, two young lovers came walking by, hand in hand, sated with the pleasures of love on a hot afternoon. They waved at the pair of hill-billies sittin' on the porch.

"You see them city folk?" Ezra queried. "They been in town on their honeymoon for the past two days, and I think they brought a bunch of ghosts with them."

"How so?" Muskie belched.

"Well, we been gettin' reports from all over these mountains of strange moanin' and groanin' goin' on."

"Well, they want to stay away from Ghost Lake," Muskie nodded.

"By the way, Muskie, where's that trout you said you caught?"

"Heck," Muskie replied. "I was admirin' that big, ol' speckled fella when that ghost started moanin' agin and said, 'Oh no! It's so big!' And this other ghost moans, 'Let go of it!' Course, I did what them ghosts said and got to hell outta there!"

Ray Dillon owns and operates Malarkey Cabin Guiding Service at Zealand, New Brunswick, and is a licensed fishing and hunting guide.

WHY DO WE FLY-FISH?
By Jim McLennan

You've probably noticed this too: people who don't fly-fish think we do it to catch fish. Silly notion, isn't it? Sometimes, catching fish is quite a ways down the priority list.

People can take several routes into our sport, but it usually happens one of two ways. Often people try fly-fishing after they've spent some time with other tackle and methods. Sometimes this transition works; sometimes it doesn't. If the person switches because he thinks fly-fishing will be more fun, it usually turns out okay.

Some people, though, switch to fly-fishing to rectify what they see as an intolerable situation–they aren't catching fish. When they're doing poorly with their spinning or casting tackle and a fly-fisherman comes along and catches a bunch of fish, they make the presumption that the reason for the other guy's success is his different tackle. They figure that once they get a fly-fishing outfit in their hands they'll immediately start catching fish the way he does. It's unfortunate (or maybe it isn't), but when these people realize that changing their tackle doesn't change their luck, most of them drop out.

While a lot of people get into fly-fishing via other methods, there are plenty of good, young fishermen around who have never done it any other way. In fact, some of these teenaged wizards already know more about fly-fishing than most of us will ever learn. Somebody obviously neglected to tell them about the years of practice the sport is supposed to require. People taking this direct route into fly-fishing are usually encouraged by a friend, and they generally do well because the friend transmits his enthusiasm and gets the newcomer excited about the sport for the right reasons.

There is actually a third category of people, or maybe it should be called a non-category. These are the ones who see a TV program of a fly-fishing video or somebody demonstrating fly casting at a sportsman's show and think it might be fun to take up the sport some day. I call these the fresh-air-and-exercise people. They think it would be healthy and pleasant, but those are more fringe benefits than major draws of the sport. There are cheaper and probably better ways of getting fresh air and exercise, such as riding a bike or playing tennis, and come to think of it, that's usually what these people end up doing. Though they have good intentions, and a fair number of them even go so far as to enrol in a fly-fishing school somewhere, they rarely stick with it.

Okay, so for whatever reason, we end up with a fly rod or two, a couple of magazine subscriptions and a membership in the local fin, fur and feather club, and we consider ourselves to be *serious* fly-fishers. What is it we like about it now that we are here? Why does this sport become so ridiculously important to so many of us? Let me review some of the more universal reasons before I tell you about my own.

Some like fly-fishing for the refuge it provides from day-to-day stress. Although I once fished with a business tycoon who insisted on frequent stream-side conversations with his Dictaphone, fly-fishing pulls most of us away from such concerns and allows us to get lost in what we're doing. It's easy to spend a whole day on the water and not once think of the office or the clock.

The beautiful places that fly-fishing takes us to are part of what many people like about it, and some crave the solitude of such places, while others feel the beauty is wasted if it's not shared with a companion. That's not as contradictory as it sounds.

The words "fly-fishing" can mean a lot of different things these days, and the sport's tremendous breadth appeals to many of us. Tiny mountain brook trout, bass, salmon, steelhead and salt-water fish bigger than the angler can all be objectives of fly-fishermen's attentions. These are different fish living in different environments, requiring different tackle and different methods, and any one of them can be worth a lifetime or two of study. I have done a lot of fly-fishing but for a relatively few species of fish, and it makes me giddy to think about all the fishing I have left to do.

Fly-fishing can lead to many other hobbies that just might become more important than the fishing itself. I know people who are more interested in tying flies than in fishing with them. Others get completely wrapped up in trout-stream entomology. In Pennsylvania, a man named Charlie Meck would far sooner sample and study the insects in the streams than fish for the trout that eat them.

Many of us began to carry a camera when we started fly-fishing, and some of us now consider that piece of equipment more essential than the rod on a fishing trip.

There's a sequence fly-fishermen often go through: they take up the fishing first, then fly tying, then they try building a fly rod from a kit. Most of us leave it there, but some look for a greater challenge and find it in the construction of split-cane rods. This is a very ambitious project, and I'm glad there are people still doing it for without them we might eventually lose ties with an important part of the history of our sport. Some builders, such as Don Andersen of Rocky Mountain House, sell a small number of rods each year, while others, such as Bob Kambeitz of Calgary and Des MacFarland of Edmonton, are content to make cane rods for themselves and a few lucky friends. At about a 100 hours per rod, these guys are spending more time in their workshops than in the water.

Fly-fishing has such a rich literary tradition that many people have become completely immersed in the history of the sport and the millions of words written about it. A friend of mine lost many valuable belongings to a basement flood, and what concerned him most was his extensive collection of fishing books.

When we're young and thirsty, we think books are important because they teach us how to catch fish. As we get older, though, books become important for a different reason--they allow us to continue our love affair with the sport after we've begun to have difficulty wading big rivers and seeing small flies.

Now let me tell about my own reasons for fly-fishing. I'm intrigued by the fact that nobody ever has, nor ever will, truly master this sport. No matter how much we think we've learned, what we don't know far outweighs what we do know. Every answer spawns three more questions. I think of fly-fishing as a trip through a tunnel. The tunnel starts out quite narrow, and our objective is simple--we just want to catch that slimy little fish. As we get further in, the tunnel begins to widen. Now we want to know why we can catch certain fish and why we can't catch others. We want to learn more about the fish's behaviour, then the behaviour of the fish's food, then the effect of water temperature on both of them. We may become wrapped up in fly casting or the theories of insect imitation or the effects of barometric pressure and the moon on the fish. Before long the tunnel is so wide we can't even see the walls any more, and we have more unanswered questions and a greater thirst for understanding than when we started.

I also like the fact that almost nothing in fly-fishing is clear-cut. What's true today might not be true tomorrow. A fish is rising in a stream, and you conclude that he's taking a particular stage of a tiny mayfly. You tie your new imitation of the emerging nymph onto a ridiculously fine leader and make a fancy cast that you learned from the latest fly-casting video. You catch the fish. You're a genius, right? Well, what if you don't catch the fish?

Worse, what if you don't catch him, but an oldtimer with a glass rod splats a size-ten Royal Coachman over there and does catch the fish? Does that make sense? Of course not. Does this kind of thing ever happen? It sure does to me, and while it drives me nuts in one way, in another way I love it.

I tell people in fishing schools that to take up fly-fishing is to agree to take the fish on under his rules. We are almost always attempting to imitate one of the fish's natural foods with our choice of fly, and are trying to make it behave like the food by the way we fish the fly. I like the idea that the fly does what it does because the fisherman makes it do it. You can't say this about other methods. Bait appeals to the fish because it is real food with taste and smell, and spoons and spinners have attractive motion designed within the lure. This is not to say that knowledge and skill won't make a bait or hardware fisherman more effective; it is to say that the skill of the angler is a greater factor in fly-fishing than in other types of fishing.

When I fly-fish, I feel I am imposing myself on the fish's world and disrupting his existence to a degree, but I balance that by telling myself that I can do it without harming the fish or his environment. In fact, I tell myself that in the big picture I am probably of benefit, because as I come to appreciate and enjoy the fish and his world, I am likely to become a staunch protector and defender of both.

A large part of why I fly-fish is to collect a batch of memories. I like to have gone fishing so I can look back and relive fishing when I'm not doing it. I have a little file in my mind that I'm trying to fill with memories of fishing experiences. Like books, these allow me to enjoy the sport whenever and wherever I choose.

In the end fly-fishing, more than any other kind, asks me to learn about the fish's world. My success is measured not by the catching of fish but by the learning. I'm fascinated by the fish, and I crave an understanding of what they're doing. I don't mind not catching them if I can feel fairly certain why. When I think I have something figured out and am able to (at least in my mind) verify it by catching the fish, I feel a great satisfaction. When my theory fails, I rethink and rescheme, and it is this that keeps me coming back. I want to know more about what exactly is going on down there, and fly-fishing is the most entertaining way I know of trying to find out.

So these are some of the reasons we like this sport. Many of them are a sort of by-product–something we appreciate after we're into the sport but didn't know when we took it up. Most of us like fishing initially for no greater reason than because it is fun to feel a fish tugging on the end of a line. After we've been at it a few years, though, these other things are what keep us at it. Notice I didn't mention catching fish very often?

Jim McLennan is a writer and photographer specializing in fly-fishing and bird hunting. He is the author of *Blue Ribbon Bow*, an examination of Alberta's Bow River. He lives in Okotoks, Alberta.

THE TWO SIDES OF SALMON FISHING
By Herb M. Curtis

One afternoon in August of last year, my phone rang.

It was my brother Gary calling from the Miramichi.

I was born and raised on the Miramichi near Blackville, but I've been living in Fredericton for about 20 years. Fredericton is a good place for an angler to live. It's situated on the St. John River at the mouth of the Nashwaak. Both the St. John and the Nashwaak have salmon runs, and the St. John can compete with the best of them when it comes to bass fishing. Also Fredericton is less than an hour's drive from the Miramichi, the greatest salmon-fishing river in the world, or so we Miramichiers believe.

My brother Gary still lives on the Miramichi, close enough that he can sit in his living room and watch the salmon leap.

"The salmon are running," he said.

"Are you sure?" I asked.

"Well, the fishing's been good for three days, and they're still picking them up downriver. I landed a 12-pounder and a grilse last evening. Dad caught a couple; Hub, Dennis and Phil have lucked out as well. It looks good."

"Okay," I said. "I'll see you in a couple of hours."

I suppose every angler knows that when he gets the message there's a run on, it's a good idea to respond quickly, for conditions can change in a matter of a day, or even a few hours. Even though fishing may have been great yesterday, today you might find yourself casting over barren waters.

I responded as quickly as I could, but as it turned out, I couldn't get away until early the next morning–early enough that I was waist-deep in the Miramichi by eight o'clock.

I recall that I was very excited, that hearing the songs of the Hardy and Phleuger reels, the comments of the fishermen, seeing the salmon and grilse leap and roll, was like entering into a fisherman's dream of Utopia.

Already there were five other guys in the pool. Gary–a master fisherman and a great fly tier–was about 80 feet downstream from me. Dennis Hennessy waded quietly upstream from me, and Bill and Phil Campbell fished toward us from the other side of the river. Hub Crawford was anchored just upstream from us in his canoe.

Dennis Hennessy had already landed and released a 15-pounder. Phil Campbell had a grilse tagged and lying in a little pool at the water's edge. Hub Crawford had one in his canoe, and Gary was slightly annoyed because he'd lost one due to a knot in his leader.

Within an hour, I too had beached a grilse and was sitting on a rock on shore smoking a cigar, not knowing at the time that the germ of this story was beginning to develop. This story, by the way, is about conversations on the river, and this particular conversation, the positive one, the one we had that morning when the fish were running and everyone was lucking out, began when a large salmon jumped not more than 10 feet away from Hub Crawford's canoe.

"Boys!" exclaimed Hub. "Did you guys see that?"

"An old timer!" yelled Phil Campbell. "A 40-pounder, I'd say."

"It's sure good to see them big ones back in the river again," commented Gary.

"Yes sir," said Hub. "We're seeing more and more of them. Thank God for the old Miramichi, eh?"

"The greatest river in the world!" said Bill Campbell, proudly. "You ever notice that the salmon from this river tastes better than the ones ya catch in other rivers?"

"There's no river like the Miramichi, that's for sure," said Dennis Hennessy. "But an Atlantic salmon is an Atlantic salmon wherever you catch it. The salmon are the king of sports fish, the greatest in the world. I heard they give you more battle per pound than any other fish, and I've never seen one yet caught on this river or any other river that wouldn't taste good with a few potatoes and a little chow-chow."

"Barney Google with the goo- goo- googilly eyes, . . . " sang Gary contentedly.

"I'd sooner fish salmon than make love," said Bill Campbell.

The boys all laughed at this comment, and I stood and started for the upper end of the pool.

"Don't bother walking 'way up there," said Dennis. "Wade right in there in front of me."

"Thank you," I said. "I just thought . . ."

"I know it's polite to go to the head of the pool, but we're all friends here. And besides, there's lots of fish to go around."

"Well, thanks very much," I said and waded in between Dennis and Gary.

"I was up to Buttermilk Brook the other day and met up with this guy from Moncton," said Dennis. "A real nice lad, staying up there all by himself in a little camper on the back of his truck. We fished all day together, he and I caught our limits, had a real good day. I told him to come down here and fish if he ever needed company."

"I rolled one!" yelled Hub.

"Boys! There's lots o' them, ain't there?" said Phil. "I just rolled one myself."

"Ha! There he is! Boys, he took that some good. Come clean out of the water for it!" Hub was into a fairly good-sized salmon.

"Ha, ha! Hold 'im high!" yelled Bill. "Hold his head up!"

"I can't believe how beautiful the river is today," I said. "I'm so glad I came over. I'd sooner be here than in any other place in the world, I think. What did you hook that fish on, Hub?"

"A green butt butterfly. Do you have one?"

"No, I don't."

"Well, as soon as I land this fish, I'll give you one. I have two of them."

"Great, great."

"I don't think them salmon care what you throw at them. They'll take anything if you cover them right," said Dennis.

"Yeah, I hooked that grilse on a bear hair," said Gary. "They'll take anything at all."

"Look! Bill rolled one! What did he come for, Bill?"

"Cosseboom!"

"Are the commercial boys catching many fish?" I asked.

"I was talking to Euclid LeBlanc, and he said they're catching their limits every day, and the Indians are doing good fishing, too."

"That's good, that's good," said Phil. "There's lots to go around."

Hub's salmon took a long run down through the pool and jumped.

"Boys! Look at him go!" yelled Gary. "Stay with him, Hub!"

I could see something swimming on the far shore. "What's that over there?" I asked.

"That's a merganser," said Gary.

"It sure is good to see all the wildlife," said Dennis. "I saw an osprey a little while ago."

"And there was an otter here yesterday," said Phil.

Hub netted his salmon, released it and began to pull the anchor.

"That's my limit!" he yelled happily. "I'll see you tomorrow morning, good buddies!"

And so the morning continued on in pretty much the same way until each one of us caught his limit and left the pool. I spent the afternoon catching up on some reading, and that evening Gary's wife, Penny, laid on one of her notorious dinners after which I turned in, calling it the end of a perfect day.

The next morning, after a hearty breakfast, Gary and I changed leaders and flies, donned our waders and vests, and headed over the hill to the pool. All the others except for Dennis were already there.

"Any luck?" yelled Gary.

"Have only been here for about a half-hour," yelled Hub from his canoe. "Haven't seen a thing, yet."

"It's early," said Phil. "You can never catch a fish until after the fog lifts, until the sun burns them bubbles off the water."

Gary and I waded in to our respective positions and began casting. We all fished quietly for about an hour before anyone spoke.

"Sure is quiet," said Hub. "I wonder why Dennis never showed up this morning?"

"I think he's saving his tags for September," said Phil Campbell. "Although he wouldn't have to worry about using the last of his 10 at this rate."

"I've been buying a licence every year since they came up with the new system, and I never ran out yet. The year before last, I never caught a fish," said Hub.

Time passed. There were no fish showing and no fish being caught. It was like fishing in a different river. The inactivity led my brother Gary to comment, "It looks like the run's over."

"What run? We only had about three days of good fishing. Ya couldn't call that a run," said Bill.

"It's sure not like what it used to be," I put in.

A stranger came over the hill and joined us. None of us knew him, but I found out later that it was the guy that Dennis had fished with at Buttermilk Brook, the guy from Moncton. Not one of us greeted him, as is often the case when a stranger enters a pool on an unproductive day.

After a while, Phil said, "I think the water might be too warm. The salmon have probably all gone to the cool waters of the brooks. What we need is a good rain."

"The wind's in the east, and when the wind's in the east, the fish bite least," said Bill.

"We'll not get any amount until after the full moon," said Hub.

"You know what I think is going on," said Gary. "It's too late for the July run and too early for the September run."

"In my recollection, there used to be bigger runs than the one we had for the past few days. I wouldn't doubt the acid rain has something to do with it," said Phil.

"I think the Indians are netting them all," said Bill.

"The poachers get more than their fair share, too," said Gary. "Not to mention those damned mergansers over there! Them things will eat their weight in parr every day!"

"I was down to Quarryville yesterday," said the guy from Moncton, "and there were so many fishermen down there that I can't see how a salmon could get up the river anyway."

Everyone ignored that comment. None of us knew this guy well enough to respect his opinion.

"I heard Tom Smith has a piano wire stretched across the river," said Hub.

"There's too much algae and not enough oxygen," was my first comment on the problem.

"We haven't had really good fishing since the flood of '76," said Bill.

"The salmon have seen so many flies that they can tell the difference between a real one and an artificial one," said Gary. "They're getting educated. Even old Everett Price couldn't fool them with his oriole or cosseboom these days."

"I never caught a fish for a long time," said the guy from Moncton.

"Do you have a big white bomber?" asked Hub.

"No," said the Monctonian.

"Too bad, for that's what they're takin'," lied Hub.

"Dog days don't help matters," said Phil. "You can never catch a salmon during dog days."

"But it's the end of the month, and fishing generally picks up at the end of the month," I said.

"A salmon just jumped down there on the bend," said the Monctonian.

"A jumping fish won't take," said Gary.

"There's a few fish around, but they're just going right through," said Hub. "The Russians are gettin' the most of them out on the high seas."

"Not to mention the Newfoundlanders," said Phil.

"And the Frenchmen downriver are getting their fair share, you can bet on that!" said Bill.

"It's sure not like it used to be," I said.

"I think my leader's too big," said Gary. "I should go down to a six."

"Mine's too short. My fly's hitting too hard," I said.

The guy from Moncton waded ashore, changed his fly and lit a cigarette. While he was smoking, Dennis Hennessy came over the hill and waded into the pool to where the Monctonian had been standing. When the Monctonian finished his cigarette, he waded out in front of Dennis.

"Where the hell you think you're going?" yelled Dennis.

"I'm sorry," said the Monctonian. "I thought . . ."

"I don't care what you thought! It's sort of an unwritten rule, if you know what I mean! When you go ashore to land a fish, or for whatever reason, you always start again at the top of the pool! It's a little courtesy, if ya know what I mean!"

"Sorry," said the Monctonian and went to the head of the pool behind Dennis.

Dennis, I suppose, was thinking that maybe he was being too hard on the Monctonian he'd had such a good day with on Buttermilk Brook. After a bit, he turned and asked, "Have you been having any luck?"

"I haven't caught a fish since Buttermilk," said the Monctonian.

"You should have been here yesterday," said Dennis.

"You know it's awful warm for the time of year," I put in. "For good fishing, we need a few cold nights."

"Ah, but the scenery's so nice," said Hub, and I detected both boredom and sarcasm. "You know where I'd like to go some day? I'd like to go up to Labrador, fish them big trout that they catch up there."

"Now that's what I'd call fun," said Gary. "Those guys up there have all the luck."

"Oh well!" sighed Bill.

"I rolled one," said the Monctonian, and every one of us turned to see if it was true. We watched him make another cast. His fly drifted across a hot spot . . .

Kersplash!!

The stranger tightened up on a salmon. His reel sang, his rod bent.

"Yahoo! Hold 'im high!"

"Keep your rod up!"

"Get the net, Bill!"

"What's your name again?"

"Joe. Joe MacDougal."

"Great fishin', eh, Joe?"

Herb M. Curtis is the author of six books including three humorous novels. He lives in Fredericton, New Brunswick.

DARK OF THE MOON
By Bob Rife

The only way to approach the opening of the angling season for pickerel (or wall-eye, if you must) is with a scientific bent. Charlie, my father-in-law, points out that my scientific bent is more stooped than bent. He mispronounces that word so it comes out "stupid."

His parting shot as I headed out to the car for the trip north to the Kawartha Lakes was, "Don't get hooked on some crazy notion, or those slickers will take you good."

What Charlie, a former resident of those northern wilds, didn't know was that I had already obtained full information on the phases of the moon, something that has a great effect on the night-feeding pickerel. They love the dark.

And as I told Percy Nichols and his son Bill, the two Bobcaygeon anglers who would be my companions out on Pigeon Lake, "Things might not be so hot for the opening. You see, there's a full moon now. That means fishing will be only fair."

Percy, a sometime guide and local politician, nodded his head. "Un-huh." There was a slight twitch at the corner of his mouth–the ghost of a smile?

I went on. "The way I've got it figured, the dark of the moon this month occurs around the Victoria Day weekend. That's about a week away. That's when the pickerel will be out in force, really snapping at the bait."

That twitch breached Percy's tanned features. It was a smile, full-blown.

"Well now," he said, "I've got just the cure for that–a new bait I've worked up, a sure killer."

I leaned forward to peer into his bait box. "Whoa now! I'm not going to show it to you until we get out there in the boat. You'll probably laugh. But I'm not worried about that, because I know it works–even in the daytime, moon or no moon."

It was a tantalizing pitch, done by a man who has been down the trail and back. I could hardly wait to see the new bait in action.

Dawn on opening day was misty. It was to be cloudy all day with the odd shower breaking the grey monotony. As we took off down the river toward the lake, Bill was at the wheel. I was in the stern working with anchor lines and doing other mate-like things. Percy sat amidships, his hands busy with tackle. He knew what he was about.

"Well," he said, "there she is." He held up a battered spinner to which was attached a trailing foil and a large, single hook. Impaled on the hook was the most splendiferous pink and purple-glittered plastic grub I've ever seen. "Now, don't laugh," Percy chided again. "She works. Looks aren't everything."

Just then he stood and pointed a little south of our position and told Bill to move inshore about 10 yards. "That's the weed bed we want."

Bill manoeuvred the boat, and I fumbled in my tackle box for an approximation of the killer lure. While we were busy, Percy made the first cast.

Two pulls and he had a fish, a big one from the way it thumped his rod. Bill grabbed the landing net, while I searched for my camera–first of the trip and on the killer lure!

The hook came loose just as the fish slipped into the net, so Bill and I were kept occupied putting the catch on the stringer–enough time to let Percy move into position and fire another cast.

In two more easy motions that looked suspiciously like jigging pulls, he had another fish. Percy manhandled this one into the boat himself, while Bill and I cast our plastic grub-decorated spinners with no success.

Percy suggested we move to another weed bed. Again while Bill cut the boat into position, and I dropped our stringer of fish over the side, Percy made the first cast.

Once again he got a strike.

This time, as Bill landed it, we noticed some black hair–deer hair– protruding around the hook in the pickerel's jaw.

I grabbed at the lure, pulling it free. "Why that's not your sure-fire killer. That's an old buck-tail jig, the ones we've always used here."

Percy's smile was a mile wide.

"You sonofagun!" I shouted. "Touting us onto that crazy-looking grub and spinner and then sitting where you could hide the old jig and get first cast!"

Percy was laughing now. "Just wanted to show you young bucks that you can sell a fisherman just about anything when it comes to a lure. And I did."

What was it that Charlie had said about being slickered?

Bob Rife is a freelance writer and photographer, and former Outdoors Editor of *The Globe and Mail* in Toronto. He lives in Scarborough, Ontario.

DOWNTOWN BROWNS
By Ross Purnell

An audible slurp seemed to indicate approval as the trout took one bug after another from the gentle surface currents. The fish seemed to be struggling against deadly buoyancy as their snouts disappeared only to bob to the surface moments later.

Several cormorants watched the feast from a dead tree. The trout were far from prey-size, and the birds showed little interest in leaving their evening silhouette.

As I strung up my rod, I pondered the likelihood of our situation. We weren't on one of those famous rivers in Montana that grace the covers of so many magazines. Neither were we on some Frenchman's creek that so many writers love to describe but hate to name. We were five minutes from my home, angling in the heart of a large urban centre.

The section of the Bow River that flows through Calgary is overshadowed by the more-famous special-regulations area that begins immediately below it. The latter area has been proclaimed by writers and users alike as one of the world's finest trout streams. This section of the river offers over 3,000 trout per mile, classic western scenery and a variety of wildlife. The city section, on the other hand, offers fewer fish, less-attractive scenery and a smaller population of wildlife. Given its proximity to paradise, it is no wonder the city is rarely fished.

On the positive side, this part of the river has fewer anglers, more access and a healthy population of hook-jawed, German descendants that I like to call downtown browns. Far from possessing the beauty of the silvery rainbow, these spotted leviathans are as ugly as alligators and almost as toothy. These fish will smash a streamer so hard, I often have to sit right down and recompose myself. While my hands shake and my knees wobble, I wonder whether the blood pounding in my ears is the result of a lost opportunity or relief at having survived such a violent encounter. Bow River sage Jim McLennan wrote in *Blue Ribbon Bow*, "If I was specifically after a large brown, I would fish the water between the Glenmore Trail Bridge and the Highway 22X Bridge."

The urban river runs from the Bearspaw Dam, at the north-west corner of town, to Highway 22X Bridge, at the south-east corner. It runs past golf courses and freeways, through natural parklands and industrial areas, straight through the city centre into the suburbs.

This part of the Bow is not your average trout stream. Dead bodies turn up occasionally. Trout find refuge behind old shopping carts. This popular dumping ground for stolen cars and unwanted pets is also home to a good population of mule deer, bald eagles and possibly the greatest variety of waterfowl in Alberta. On weekends the river is host to everything from canoes to jet skis. Strange odours emanate from storm sewers, and strange people wander the banks. The most irritating of these are the curious onlookers who accost you from a distance and demand a response. "Any luck?" If I were fast asleep with a bell on the end of my rod, I might be depending on luck.

Instead I just shake my head or say, "No, not much." This avoids the inevitable follow-up question to the "Yes" answer: "Let's see 'um." That request requires valuable use of fishing time to explain the conservation values involved in catch-and-release fishing, followed by a blank look of disbelief or outright confrontation. "No, not much," is the easy way out.

Sometimes having observers is an added bonus. I remember a companion who hooked and played a large trout right at the tee box of a city golf course. He performed wonderfully for the golfers waiting to tee off. When the fish was brought to the net, the golfers cheered and came over for a close inspection of the catch. Most seem astonished that a 25 inch trout could be caught at the eighth hole.

The Bow River is a wide, shallow river once it gets out of the foothills. Deep, dark holes are there, but they are the exception. Most of the water is oxygen-rich riffles punctuated with pockets, corners, rocks, fallen trees and undercut banks. Generally it is this character water near the banks that holds the fish. Anglers who look for their fish near the banks will find them. Those who probe the middle of the river are likely to be disappointed.

I think of the river as a clean, blue place, kind of like those beer commercials with outdoorsy men, scantily clothed women and polar bears.

There are times, however, when the water is brown and overrunning its banks. The culprits are usually the tributaries that enter the Bow inside the Calgary city limits–Fish Creek and the Elbow River.

In keeping with this trend, the Elbow ran dirty for a good part of July 1993. The main stem of the Bow above the Elbow was relatively clear and provided some decent fishing between the Bearspaw Reservoir and Fort Calgary. Instead of sitting home griping about the river conditions, we were hammering big browns and loving every minute of it. Unfortunately many people don't realise that, generally, the farther upstream you go, the clearer a river will get.

The city portion of the river offers nearly unlimited access to every inch of bank. Its better half is problematic for fishermen on foot due to limited access to a riverside barricaded by private property. Drift-boat anglers intending to float have limited options due to the distances between government accesses. A couple of spare hours translates into an outing in the city easier than a trip to the special-regulations area.

Speaking of regulations, in this section there is no bait restriction and a two-trout limit. The result? Besides a decreased total population, brown trout seem to outnumber rainbow about four to one. In the bait-ban area, rainbow are more common. It seems as though the wily old brown is not just anthropomorphic. The sophisticated European fish seem less likely to fall prey to well-presented night crawlers than their North American cousins.

The city trout seem to have adjusted their lifestyles to combat the mentality of the average urban angler. On a sunny day, there will be gangs of people congregated at a few popular spots. The spot near the zoo and several other specific locations near parking lots are host to what I call a fishing party. This is a social event more than anything else. These people seem to enjoy people as much as fishing. They subscribe to the common belief that where there are people fishing, the fishing must be good. In reality, just the opposite is true. The most-obvious water in the city is usually the least productive. Fish do not enjoy a steady bombardment of worms and hardware. They don't hang around long in these spots. I have never seen anyone catch a thing in these spots, but I suppose it must happen. Walk a hundred yards in either direction and you will have beautiful water all to yourself. What's more, there are probably a few big trout in the vicinity.

Not only do the browns avoid well-known fishing hot spots, but they seemingly cease feeding when the sun is out. I don't know if this is a purely biological aversion to sunlight or if they have equated the sun with the presence of the fair-weather fishermen. I prefer an overcast day for fishing almost any river, but on this stretch you haven't got a chance on a bright afternoon. If it's rainy and windy and cold, those finicky giants turn suicidal. It only seems right. Anyone who fishes in that kind of weather deserves to catch them.

The best substitute for poor weather is darkness. At the end of those dog days, the fish attempt to make up for a full day of abstinence. It is said that big browns feed all night. I can't say for sure if they do or not, but I've had some great fishing up to 1 a.m. Any fish that feeds at 3 a.m. is safe from me –or is he? Stumbling back to the Jeep, with my companion releasing well-sprung branches from the blackness in front of me, I wondered what I wouldn't do to catch a huge trout. The list was painfully short.

Greg offered me first crack at the group of feeding trout that night. I knew I was supposed to pick off the bottom one first, but instead I tossed my dry fly up into the middle of the pack. "Let them fight for it," I thought to myself. Sure enough, my floating fur-and-feather apparition disappeared, and I tightened the line. The fish tried to jump, but its bulk prevented it from getting airborne. What was supposed to be an acrobatic event turned into a kind of comical wallowing. Then the line went slack.

I began to reel in. According to fly-fishing protocol, I missed my chance, and it was now my partner's turn to cast at whatever, if anything, was left. Generously Greg told me to stay put. I'm not sure if his request was the result of pity or if I was supposed to politely decline. I chose the former and began casting.

My next trout was securely hooked, and as the end of my fly line disappeared into the darkness, Canada Day fireworks lit up the opposite horizon. Greg netted the two-foot trout for me after a battle that ended a hundred yards downstream. The fish was a thick, golden male. His straight-edge tail was a perfect contrast for the face that gave him true character. His twisted jaw gave him the look of a veteran who had survived many battles on the spawning redds. In the fish world, this guy would be a major badass. Although deformed, the toothy jaws fit together with the deadly jigsaw precision of a steel trap.

The next fish was Greg's. He fought a similar-sized trout to the exact spot where we had just released mine. Unfortunately my premature lunge in the dark wasn't nearly as successful, and I karate chopped his leader with my landing net.

I don't know if the offered "Whoops!" was particularly soothing, but he didn't kill me that night, and we still fish together.

Ross Purnell is an avid fisherman who lives in Blairmore, Alberta.

IN THE HANDS OF AN EXPERT
By David E. Scott

The 10 pound brown trout got away. Let's get that fact right up front, in this story about a most unusual fishing trip, and be done with it.

It was just after 11 p.m., and fishing guide extraordinaire Mike Scott had pulled out the last stop in his effort to help the Canadian visitor catch a trophy-sized trout. Scott operates Ty-llyn Fishing Lodge on Lake Rotorua on New Zealand's North Island, two blocks from the head of what is probably the world's best trout-fishing river. He boasts that any guest catching a brown trout weighing less than eight pounds does not pay for that day's accommodation, meals and guide service.

"There will be one under the bank there, just below that little bush that sticks out. Drop your fly about one-third of the way across the river with enough line to drift it a couple of feet below that hole. Then bring it slowly up–but not too slowly or the current will take it into the bank, and you'll snag those bushes."

I knew this was it. The fish weren't rising, and Scott said nobody had caught anything for several weeks. I had worked the upper half of the river in late afternoon on my own, and for the past two hours, Scott and I had been beating the waters again. He'd shown me several dozen hidey-holes, but nothing had come roiling up out of them.

To reach this last-chance hole, we had tiptoed down a private driveway lined with No Trespassing signs. Scott assured me he had permission from the owner to use the private property to gain access to the river, but we must be careful not to wake the residents.

Close to an open bedroom window, we had to scale a smooth brick wall about six feet high to get to the river bank. We somehow managed this silently in the dark while wearing chest waders without breaking the fly rods, ripping the waders or slipping into the deep, black, fast water.

I worked the line out across the river to a length that would exactly reach the precise spot I had to land the wet fly, and then made the cast.

"Well done," came a deep-voiced whisper from somewhere in the darkness. "Perfect."

Fly-fishing is an art form. It's a passion, a way of life for some, and it can be every bit as much a snob sport as falconry or fencing. For a bumbling colonial who grew up thrashing the waters of northern Quebec with a $10 split-bamboo fly rod, that simple "well done" was enough to make the whole expedition worthwhile. The words came, after all, from the world's third-ranked fly-fisherman.

The fly snaked out and settled on the water like dandelion fluff. My eyes couldn't follow its drift in the darkness, but by gauging the current, I knew when it was in position and started to retrieve it.

The fish hit exactly where Scott said it would and exactly how he said it would–like a Mack truck.

I struck. It was like setting the hook in a tractor tire mired on the river bottom.

And then the line went slack. The leader had parted from the line. It must have snapped, because the world's third-ranked fly-fisherman, who had rigged my rod, would most definitely have tied the proper knot . . .

The angry trout jumped half a dozen times after that in the middle of the river, trying to shake the hook.

And that's how we know it weighed exactly 10 pounds.

David E. Scott is the author of five guidebooks to Ontario and editor of this anthology. He lives in Ailsa Craig, Ontario.

MAC 'N' ME
By Ray Dillon

The morning dawned as clear as the atmosphere in the local bingo hall on a Wednesday evening. There were blue clouds, grey clouds, dark clouds and threatening clouds all jostling each other for position in the sky as we walked silently towards the river.

There was Mac, a big old lad of 76 years, trudging ahead of me with his dog Charmer. Mac was an old warhorse fishing New Brunswick for the first time, and I was to be his guide for the week. It would prove to be a most eventful five days of fishing . . .

Mac was almost totally deaf in both ears and although a charming man of considerable wealth, was obsessed by frugality. Well, the fact is, he was cheap. Damned cheap. His older brother had recently passed on to that big salmon pool in the sky, and as it happened, had been the proud owner of two ancient hearing aids to which Mac laid claim at the funeral. "No use in buryin' him with them," he had grinned. So on this dark morning in July, he stumbled towards the salmon pool with white, plug-like things sticking out of both ears.

"Mac," I yelled, "watch out for those big rocks down by the pool. They're slippery."

"Yeh, I got my flies with me," he replied.

Those hearing aids were remarkably effective.

Charmer–a grave misnomer for that ugly dog–was having his morning constitutional on the pathway, and old Mac stumbled right onto his leavings, slipping and doing a wild half-gainer with a twist before thudding to the ground. Being Mac's guide, I hustled to his side, concerned he might have broken my graphite fishing rod.

"Whew! I guess it's okay," I sighed with relief.

"Oh yes, I'm okay. Just tripped over something," Mac said.

The thunder began rumbling in the north-east and lightning flashed across the sky as we arrived at the pool. Old Charmer, bless his heart, spotted a couple of big salmon lying near the shore beside a large rock and quickly splashed out to move them. As Mac and I prepared fishing lines, the mutt charged back between us to shake himself off, giving both of us a shower.

The old man reached down and gently patted the dog's head. "Good Charmer; good dog."

Charmer came over to me, and I patted his head also, but slightly harder. "I'm gonna drown you, dog, first chance I get," I mumbled.

Mac looked up then, and for a moment I feared he'd overheard. He looked at the dog and then straight at me. "Yeh, Charmer, tell him. Tell him that you do like to swim."

The thunder rumbled closer, and the lightning flashes were preceding the roars by mere seconds. I urged Mac to stop casting and head back to the truck. He refused, smacking me right between the eyes on his back swing with a number-four Double Copper Killer–appropriate name for a fly. I promptly moved back to Mac's side.

The safest place to be in an electrical storm is under cover, inside a vehicle or low to the ground. Streamside with a graphite lightning rod/fishing pole in hand courts disaster. I could see it coming. God was casting lightning bolts, and they were heading our way. Maybe it was the cork handle or the fact that Mac stood on a rock that saved him that morning, but when the jagged bolt hit his forward-casting rod, I could see the charge come sizzling down the pole and jump off into the water. Mac stood motionless on the rock, his white, mid-length hair standing on end in a huge Afro. His eyes were slightly glazed, but that seemed natural–possibly his medication. His entire form appeared to glow slightly. As he turned to step down, determined to make the shoreline, he fell in slow motion, and I jumped to catch him. His 215 pounds hit me like a wet sack of bones, and I found myself lying on the rocks beneath him, my face half submerged in water. As I struggled to get up, the rain dumped down in sheets. I honestly believe that to this day, Mac doesn't know I was his gym mat on that fateful morning.

Mac was halfway to the truck by the time I picked up my bruised and bleeding body from the water's edge. Old Charmer, oblivious of the rain, had been washing my face with the same tongue he had just used to wash his private parts. "Get away, you son of a -----," I moaned and struggled up the path to the truck where Mac turned to survey me.

"What you doin' down there in that storm? Did you see that bolt of lightning? Hell, I almost fell and hurt myself on those rocks. Did you see me fall?"

I wiped blood from one of my hands and the side of my face and spat out some sand. I looked at the old fisherman with his wild, long eyebrows and hair on end, appearing not unlike the mad scientist who had just discovered he's created Frankenstein. "Let's get in out of the rain and have a coffee," I smiled.

Over the next hour and a half, we sat and listened to the rain beat on the windshield and roof. We talked about many things. Well, I talked about some things, and he'd reply about others, entirely different. We discussed flies, me seeking common ground and him pretending to hear every word. I'd lean over and yell, "The Green Machine is a good fly for this river, Mac."

"Yeh, Charmer's okay. He never even got his feet wet."

"I wasn't talking about the dog," I'd yell.

"Was there a fish laying out by that log?" he'd reply.

The rain eventually abated, and the sky began to clear. Patches of blue showed with white, puffy clouds coming in from the north-east. A stiff, gusty breeze gave the salmon pool a shivery look. Mac's guttural voice resounded down the river-bank as he yelled for Charmer. The darned dog was trotting about marking what he believed to be his territory, and that included every bush, tree and tire in sight. He paid absolutely no attention to Mac.

"What a well-behaved dog he is," I remarked as we headed for the river once more.

Mac looked around at me, pretending to have understood every word and grinned. "Yeh, I'll go out and fish by that log."

For an old man he moved remarkably fast and was soon up to the top seam of his chest waders. "Can't cast from here," he complained. I rushed into the cool water, splashing noisily. "Hell, it's deep near that log. I don't think I can make, . . . " his voice trailed off into bubbles and gurgling sounds, and all I could see of Mac was his beige fishing hat, floating, some ripples and the tip of his rod.

I rushed to retrieve him.

Now this is not amusing. In fact, it's downright scary when you've got an old man, more than 200 pounds of senility and stubbornness, fighting your every move.

I recovered Mac but not without swallowing some of the river and certainly not without bodily injury–to me. As we crawled from the tea-coloured water, Mac coughed and sputtered something about my ability to guide, and why would I send him out into the deep water by the log? I bit my lip and limped quietly on the bruised leg he'd trampled while flailing about. Mercifully the day eventually ended.

We watched the sun come up next morning as we bounced along in my old van, driving into another wilderness salmon pool. Charmer was in the back for most of the ride, but occasionally he'd come up front to stick his nose out the window. "He's a good bird dog," Mac would grunt, gently patting the mutt's head. Charmer would respond by giving Mac's old, worn face a lick or two. Then the dog would swing over to me.

"Get in the back, you disgusting piece of dog flesh," I'd growl.

Mac would look over and ask, "Did he howl last night? I didn't hear him?"

The ride was uneventful, and nobody spoke during the next couple of miles until Mac announced we were approaching a big hill. This puzzled me since there were only slight undulations in the road ahead. I looked over at this man who had so many health problems, quickly turned back and hung my head out the window. In addition to being almost stone deaf, Mac couldn't see very well and had poor depth perception. So the old, re-tired soldier gazed ahead through the windshield with a large pair of 10X binoculars, barely keeping them against his eyes. Every now and then, they'd slam back and hit his forehead or the bridge of his nose.

I laughed, out of control at first, and when I thought I had a grip on it, turned to him. "Mac, it's those glasses that are making you see big hills and valleys."

"Damned hard to see when you're going over those bumps so fast," he shot back. I doubt if he heard what I'd said. He swung the binos around to peer at Charmer and me, and once again I had to turn and look out my window, catching bugs in my teeth.

Soon the gentle shimmer of silver in the morning sunlight indicated our pool was straight ahead. It would be a relief to be streamside once again.

The week went by without Mac hooking into a fish until the last day. Mac had hooked both Charmer and me on several occasions; he could snare us no matter where we tried to hide.

Actually the best action I saw that week was when Mac sunk a double number four Orange Blossom Special into Charmer's backside and thought he had hooked a fish. Mac felt the line stiffen and set the hook just as Charmer decided this thing hurt. There was a howl, and Charmer jumped right into the shallow water on poolside.

Down along the pool went the dog, leaping, howling and splashing. Mac stood on the rod, causing it to bow. "You hooked the dog, Mac!" I yelled.

"Yeh, Charmer, don't chase that fish!" he called to the crazed dog.

"No, Mac! You hooked *into* the dog! The *dog* has been hooked!"

"Oh, don't worry, Ray, Charmer won't hurt the fish. He's all trained, yuh know," Mac roared.

All the while, Charmer was trying to rid himself of that hook, and he'd moved into deeper water, jumping, barking, splashing and yelping frantically.

I could see the dog needed my help since Mac, handicapped by his short-sightedness, couldn't distinguish between fish and dog. I rushed to him. Well, maybe I didn't rush. Charmer, after all, wasn't exactly my favourite pooch, and it was difficult for me to see Mac because of the tears of laughter streaming down my face.

Eventually, though, I wrestled the rod from Mac's hands and gave Charmer some slack. He came when I commanded–especially whenever I reefed on the rod.

An hour later, Charmer sat in the van, and I was releasing a 12 pound Atlantic salmon. Mac was ecstatic.

I had moved up considerably in his estimation, from a coarse, uncaring, unknowledgeable, New Brunswick, licensed guide, to a coarse, uncaring guide who knew a bit about hooking salmon. It had been a memorable week, and believe it or not, Mac brought Charmer back to bird hunt with us that autumn.

Over the years, Mac and I became good friends based on conversations and experiences that probably only the good Lord can fathom.

Mac returns to fish with me every year, and Charmer comes with him. Between hooking both of us and attempting to drown me on several occasions, we plod on. Our bird hunts are quite unbelievable, but at least I don't have scars from a double number-four hook when our week is over.

Mac's getting older, and I know he's closing on that path that leads to the great outdoors scene in the sky.

I believe that in heaven, we'll be able to hunt and fish in comfort. We won't have to worry about game that got away or how bad the flies are when we're fishing. I just hope and pray that if they use guides up there, Mac gets one with a lifetime warranty on his soul. Guiding Mac for a week can wear pretty thin on a guy, and cause a sober man to start drinkin'.

Ray Dillon owns and operates Malarkey Cabin Guiding Service at Zealand, New Brunswick, and is a licensed fishing and hunting guide.

SECOND SHOT AT A FIRST BASS
By Wil Wegman

It isn't often that we get a second chance to relive historic moments in our lives. And those memories do fade. How many dedicated bass fanatics can remember that very first bass? And how many get a second shot at that very special moment?

I had the chance this summer after meeting my cousin Cees (pronounced Case) for the first time while he was visiting from his native Holland. Although he's been an ardent angler for 40 years, bass were unknown to him. When I recovered from the shock of learning a relative of mine knew little or nothing about this most-exalted fish, a feeling of pity set in. After all Cees couldn't be blamed for the fact that Holland is a deprived, bassless nation.

My bass-crazed brother Red and I decided the best cure for our cousin's life-without-bass affliction was to rush him into a bass boat for a crash course on what real fishing was all about.

Cees wasn't so sure. In his European style of fishing, live bait led the way in most cases. "What you mean? You bring no worms, minnows, grasshoppers or, best of all, maggots?"

"Ugh! No way, cuz. You'll just have to adapt to our fake-bait techniques if you want to catch your bass with us." Okay, I did stretch the truth a bit and tell him that bass wouldn't take live bait, but I figured what he didn't know wouldn't hurt him and the artificials would be a new and interesting experience for him.

We began our quest for his first bass in a small southern-Ontario lake, a lake that usually produces plenty of largemouth. We threw artificials all morning, but the bass action was uncharacteristically slow. Red caught a couple of nice bass on a Dying Flutter, and I got a few on a Kangaroo Worm, but poor old Cees was still bassless.

He did, though, manage to catch a number of pike on spinner baits. He'd caught European pike, but he'd taken them on live bait and had never in his life taken a fish on anything resembling a spinner bait. That at least was a first, even if it wasn't a first bass.

Cees really wasn't convinced that admiring our bass was as good as catching them himself. In fact, he was becoming somewhat anxious about boating a bass of his own, so we decided to switch lakes. Oddly enough, we were headed for the mouth of the Holland River on Lake Simcoe; the name alone might just be enough to change his luck.

Our mission was to introduce Cees to a more fulfilling life through bassing, even if we had to stay out all day and all night to do it. This was prime flippin' territory, undercut banks topped by cattails all along the shoreline. And there was enough timber mixed with floating slop to give Cees a good idea of the country Mr. Largemouth likes to call home.

Cees insisted on sticking with familiar spinning gear. He had never encountered bait casters before and figured the artificial lures were handicap enough without wrestling with new tackle. He said he'd just watch us flip for a few minutes and then mimic us with his own gear. It took some time, but when Red and I started to connect with bass, we had ourselves a ball. Cees was having a tough time of it, hitless despite his best efforts. After Red and I had released about a dozen bass, I convinced Cees, with little effort, that he ought to at least have a stab at the bait casters if he was going to continue flippin'.

I led him through the steps of the flippin' procedure and then handed over my Shimano Flippin' Stick. He let seven feet of line hang below the rod tip and then peeled another seven feet and grasped it in his outstretched left hand. Using the underhand pendulum motion that flippin' nuts know and love, he began to work the jig and pig. In no time at all, he had the hang of it. I got a kick out of watching the intense concentration etched on his face. Cees was good and ready for that first bass.

Fifteen minutes later, Cees began to tense up even more. He was either consumed by hunger pangs and stomach cramps or something interesting was about to happen. It was a relief to see him drop the rod tip, take up the slack and set the hook with a powerful upward sweep of the rod. Nothing slow about our boy Cees.

"Ya! Ya! I have one! I have one!" He was as excited as a kid. Right off the bat, the fish sought the refuge of a fallen tree, but Cees expertly worked it out into the open. It broke water once, splashing madly. Cees shouted with laughter as he battled the fish he so desperately wanted.

When he worked the fish alongside the boat, I slipped the net underneath and eased it aboard. What a moment! Cees had done it! He'd caught his first largemouth bass. And darned if it didn't pull the Normark digital scale down to 3.10 pounds, a nice bass in anyone's book and taken while flippin', too. Cees was justifiably proud as he held up the fish for a couple of photos.

Without another word he bent over and gently slipped that special fish back into the Holland River. The bass twisted and darted away for cover, oblivious of its impact on Cees. But even the most-hardened bass fiend can likely understand just how emotional that moment had been.

To prove to us that Bass Number One had been no fluke, Cees promptly nailed a couple more with the flippin' technique. He was an angler transformed. In fact, he was so hooked on bass fishing that Red and I later became worried about what might happen to him if he didn't get to go bassin' again. Plans were made in a hurry to fish Lake Couchiching. Cees heaved a sigh of relief. He was going to get another shot at it.

This mission's objective was a little different: to have Cees experience the all-natural high of *small*mouth action. Could he catch his first smallmouth, too? Would the first largemouth and then the first smallmouth within a couple of days be too much excitement?

The huge rock slabs that shingled the bottom of the lake were awe-inspiring to Cees. He revelled in the contrast between the crystal-clear Couchiching water and the opaque water he fishes in Holland's canals.

We started with top water baits, but only Red and his lucky prop lure could fool those finicky smallmouth. I eventually got into some nice fish on a Rattlin' Rap, but the action soon slowed to a crawl.

Things were not looking good for Cees and his first smallie. I think he was just trying to make Red and me feel better when he assured us he was content to simply watch us catch those beautiful fish on this beautiful water. It might have been nice out there, but nothing compared to actually catching those smallmouth. As he commented wistfully on the spectacular runs and leaps, my heart began to bleed for him. He wasn't fooling anyone. He wanted a smallie of his own.

If that was going to happen, Red and I had to figure out a pattern for those fish that would work for Cees. I tied on a black-and-grey Kangaroo Lizard and began tossing it in earnest. When I felt the pick-up, I set the hook and eventually boated a four-pounder. My cousin's reserved attitude and professional contentment at watching us land fish went right out the window.

In desperation he was even willing to try a Kangaroo Lizard, "the crazy-lookin' plastic t'ing. Ya! Now you have one of dose t'ings for me, ya?"

I tried to explain that it takes a lot of practice to take a fish on plastics. I told him how hard it was to detect the pickup and to time the hook set. I could handle the begging, but the tears in the corners of his eyes were really starting to get to me.

"Look," he said, "is my name Wegman, or not?" That did it. There is no use arguing with a Wegman. I showed him how to Texas-rig the lizard and how to work it through the water.

"Set the hook very hard," I instructed, "if you feel a tap, the slightest tap or if you see the line move to the side even a little bit."

"Ya! Ya! I do dat!" Cees made cast after cast, working the lizard slowly over the rocks and through the long coontail plants. Finally I saw a twitch in his line, but before I could say a word, he'd made contact with his fish.

There was never a doubt that Cees was tied into his first-ever smallmouth. The jump happened immediately and must have been three feet above the water. My cousin's eyeballs bulged, but he handled the fish perfectly. The remaining acrobatic leaps and strong, solid runs tested his skills, but after a great battle he led the weary bronzeback alongside the boat.

In a soft, polite manner, Cees asked if he could land the bass on his own, without the use of a net. Red and I watched as he lipped the two-and-a-half-pounder and swung it into the boat. I swear that his eyes were misty as he held up the bass for a brief photo session. Even before his visit to Canada, Cees was a firm believer in the catch-and-release philosophy. As I watched him allow his first-ever smallmouth to swim free, I heard him whisper reverently, "Ya. Maybe I catch you next time I come to Canada." This time there was mist in my eyes.

Once again Cees set out to prove that his first smallmouth was no accident. Four more decent smallies fell victim to his slow-moving lizard. But the highlight came when he "crossed the eyes" of a monster smallmouth, a fish that might have weighed six pounds.

"Ya! Ya! Ya! Oh boy! It's big! Ya! Ya! Ya!" he shouted almost hysterically. Then sheer disaster struck. That big, fat, lovely bass leaped for the sky and threw the hook.

One day I'll have to ask Cees to translate all those Dutch words for me. He used them once he realized that bass of a lifetime was gone for good. They aren't part of the Dutch vocabulary my mother taught me. And Cees wasn't very understanding when I patiently explained that losing the fish had added a great deal to his bass-fishing experience. That's a definite part of every bass fanatic's stockpile of memories. Come to think of it, as I rummage around the attic of my mind digging out magic moments with bass, I find that I definitely remember more of the ones that I lost than the ones I successfully boated.

Disappointment over that fish aside, it had been a great pair of fishing days for the three of us. For Cees it was the thrill of his first encounter with two magnificent members of the bass family. For Red and me, it was a priceless opportunity to relive our own first encounters of the bassin' kind.

Our trips with Cees started out with fun in mind, but Red and I discovered more. As deep as our love for our favourite kind of fishing may be, it doesn't burst onto us in full bloom. It takes time and care and nurturing and the help of others. Introducing someone, adult or child, to the passion that angling brings to our lives makes our own experiences even more intense.

Wil Wegman is a freelance, outdoors writer and Pro Bass tournament angler and owner of amBASSador Angling Services. He lives in Bradford, Ontario.

WAS THE WATER TOO HIGH?
By Wayne Curtis

The sky grew lighter. I paced the verandah floor of my log cabin while waiting for my brother Win. He was supposed to have picked me up at daybreak to begin our fishing trip on the lower reaches of the Cains River.

For months we had discussed the trip, and on this cool September morning, I was bubbling with anticipation. We would drive the 10 miles up to Shinniks Corner, put in the canoe and run down the Cains to its mouth. From there we would continue back down the main south-west Miramichi to my cabin–about 15 miles of river in all.

The fog was dense on the Miramichi that morning. I could hear the occasional splash of a jumping fish and the echo of a paddle bumping against a canvas canoe as someone went out into the Home Pool. The only other sound was the distant clatter and bang of an early-morning pulp truck on the stony road that led to the Cains.

Either I am over-anxious or he has overslept, I said to myself as I paced like an expectant father. Finally Win's station wagon, with canoe on top and lights beaming through the fog, bobbed across the elm-tree interval to the Oriole camp, and we were soon on our way.

I'd been fishing the Miramichi since the days of the log drives, but I had never run the Cains. I had always heard the older guides, including Win, talking about the Cains River runs. Many local fishermen take this trip in the autumn since this is a late river. I had seen as many as a dozen canoes drift by our camp in a single Sunday evening in September.

As we readied our canoe on Doug Cashin's shore, a large hookbill salmon broke water in slow motion. Although we were anxious to get moving, Win insisted on trying this salmon with a cast. As I stood in the canoe, he made a short cast downstream, checking for distance. Then he laid the Sunday punch right on the money, as they say.

With foam still heavy on the water from the September dew, the old hookbill bobbed his head out and seized Win's Copper Killer. A good 17 pounds, he jumped twice. I was running with the net when the hook flew out on a head shake. We were left standing disillusioned in the tall grass.

It was about eight o'clock when we finally pushed off.

About 90 per cent of the Cains is open water, so we didn't have to worry about taking someone's resting fish. There are a few private pools, though, and these we edged through, paddling close to shore so as not to disturb anything.

On many bends the river is narrow and fast. We tried the most-likely spots, pools with names like Oxbow and Whirlpool. By 9:30 I had a 10-pounder, hooked on a Silver Grey in a narrow channel at the foot of an island.

After a late breakfast of bacon and eggs cooked over a hardwood fire, some refreshments to ward off the chill and a poem or two from the Robert Service book, we moodily paddled through the afternoon. Having made good time, we did more fishing as the day wore on. We tried a few casts over the Pigeon Ledge Pool, Salmon Brook, Buttermilk Brook and the Long Hole Rapids, with only the occasional rise.

Eventually the sun began to sink behind the hills, leaving the river shaded and making it seem closer to evening than it really was. We decided we would have lunch at the Slide Pool. While I was preparing the chilli, Win hooked a small salmon and beached it after a short struggle.

From this point down, the water was fast. We passed through the Hydro Pool, Brophy Pool and Hell's Gate Rapids. Soon we were looking at the church steeple at Howards, at the mouth of the Cains.

Another half-hour, and we were back at the Home Pool. With only about 20 minutes of fishing time left, we decided to fish out the remaining daylight in this vacant piece of water.

I chose to wade on the north side, as I always do. Win pushed the canoe across to within about 40 feet of the opposite shore and dropped the anchor. I cast a lazy, Rat-faced McDougal near Poppa's Rock in the centre of the pool where the water boiled. When the dry fly swung in the boil, a 14-pound hen fish came up, took my fly and headed across the river, burning my fingers on the line.

As she headed straight toward Win's canoe, I remembered the anchor rope and yelled, "Fish on!" The salmon was still gathering speed, and I could feel her coming toward the surface, as though to jump. Sure enough about two feet this side of the canoe, the salmon leaped, splashing water on Win and landing on its belly in the middle of the canoe. Win had turned around to pull the anchor but quickly fell on the thrashing fish and wrestled it down. He now had three salmon in the canoe: my limit of two fish and his one.

He removed my hook from the fish and dropped the fly over the side. As I reeled in the skipping Rat-face, which was swinging deeper in the pool, another fish rolled and grabbed it. Since I already had my limit of two for the day, I tried my best to lose this one, a grilse. With my rod held straight out in front of me, and giving him slack, I shook the rod when he jumped. But no go; the fish stayed on.

Quickly I reached down and tailed him, and without taking the grilse from the water, released the fly. The fish swam away.

I sat down on the shore to have a smoke and relive the sudden events. Father came down to check the canoes. He looked around the shore and bar for a minute, saw nothing and turned to me.

"No fish tonight, Wayne," he said. "Water's too high."

Wayne Curtis is a freelance writer and author of *Currents in the Stream, One Indian Summer, Fishing the Miramichi* and *The Growing Seasons*. He lives in Newcastle, New Brunswick.

TROPHY FISH HAD A FLIP SIDE
By David E. Scott

We'd heard so many stories of the fabulous sport fishing in Scandinavia that we bought a lot of new and expensive equipment before going. Rainwear would have been a better investment; it rained every day. But that doesn't deter an angler, so my rod was ready when the right moment arrived.

Just north of Stjørdalshalsen, Norway, I swerved the car into a rutted lay-by, waking my companion. Wendy is not a dedicated tourist or fisherperson. In Holland she had stayed awake long enough to see one windmill; in Norway she had stayed awake long enough to see a reindeer.

"Do we have a flat tire?" she asked.

"No. We're here."

"Where? . . . All I can see is fog and rain."

"We just passed a fantastic fishing spot."

"Good luck," she murmured, snuggling into her blanket.

The fishing spot belonged on the cover of an angler's magazine–except editors don't use cover photos that show fog and horizontal rain. A small river leaped from dark mountains into a deep pool, which emptied over a set of rapids into the Atlantic. The tide was coming in. The pool was ringed with low bushes, and there were no overhanging tree branches to trap a wind-tossed lure.

Two men were working nearby on fish nets spread over a small boat. I returned their friendly waves, and they walked over as I dug through my tackle box. We couldn't communicate with words, but one of them pointed to a Red Devil lure, bobbing his head enthusiastically to indicate it was my best bet.

I waited until they left before clipping on a two-inch silver Williams Wobbler. There isn't a fish anywhere in the world of the size I wanted that can't be suckered by one of these.

I snagged some seaweed on the first cast, and a heather bush on the second–wasn't used to the feel of the new rod. The two natives watched my every move from down by their boat.

The fifth cast dropped the Wobbler precisely where I knew a monster was lurking with its mouth open and was rewarded by a snap. Not a strike; the fish simply hooked itself and headed for deep water. My new reel screamed, and I cranked the drag. It didn't slow that fish. Its first plunging run was at least 50 yards. I scampered down the bank regaining line in case it continued in the same direction, but it sulked at the bottom away downstream.

I decided to play a waiting game. With four pound test line you don't get impatient with a 20-pound fish–not if you want to see its eyeballs.

The two men ran up as I kept steady pressure on my fish. One grabbed my line and began pulling it in hand over hand, jabbering excitedly. How can you convey to a commercial fisherman–in a language he doesn't understand–that the reason you're not just cranking in the fish is because you want to play it until it is tired, which is what the sport of fishing is all about?

My fish was 10 yards from shore when it broke water–a beauty, easily 20 pounds. It made another run but my "helper" gave it line, paying it out by hand. When the fish ended its run the man eased it back to shore.

I was on the verge of hysterics and probably foaming at the mouth. Both of the men were now working my line.

Well, they did land "my" fish. Very skilfully. As one drew it close to shore the other stepped into the water and got a finger deep into a gill as the fish gasped. My prize, a lovely salmon, lay gasping in its splendour on the bank. My colleagues pressed friendly handshakes on me, and indicated the fish would make good eating. I imagined Wendy changing her tune about my lust for expensive fishing equipment when we had thick salmon steaks on the grill that night instead of pork chops at $6 each.

My fish dinner flipped just then–a great heave that turned it over. My companions grabbed at the fish uttering cries of dismay. Its entire other side was a mass of open, bloody sores and growths of vivid white fungus.

One of the men tore my lure from the fish's jaw, shouting what sounded like oaths, and booted my trophy back into the river where it disappeared like a raindrop. The fishermen explained–I think–that the fish wouldn't have been good to eat.

That was the only fish I saw anywhere during our two-week fishing tour of Scandinavia.

Wendy–who saw neither the fishermen nor my catch–has an irritating habit of occasionally referring to our $5,000 Scandinavian fishing trip and "Dave's fish that got away."

David E. Scott is the author of five guidebooks to Ontario and editor of this anthology. He lives in Ailsa Craig, Ontario.

TULLY'S POND
By Ron Miller

Old man Tully's John Deere didn't have a muffler, and that was good because the kid could hear it coming nearly a mile away. Crouched behind a patch of pond-side cattails, he watched as the old man slammed the tractor into road gear, and angrily shaking a fist, careered across his lush Indiana pastureland. At the last moment, the kid snatched up his old Gep spring-steel casting rod and his bean can of soft craws and lit out for the sanctuary of the nearby cornfield.

Some said Clyde Tully had a brass Civil War spyglass that he used to see who was trespassing on his land or fishing in his pond, but the fear of detection or the lecture which was sure to follow just wasn't enough to keep the kid from trying to catch the biggest bass he had ever seen.

The kid's folks were good neighbours and had warned him repeatedly to stay away from Tully's pond, and to confine his angling activities to the muddy little creek that flowed through their own property. That meant he was limited to the creek's meagre population of sunfish, bullheads and horny-nosed chub. But the kid had seen the great, red-eyed she-bass finning quietly in the shallows of the pond, and the chance of catching the biggest smallmouth in the county drew him to its muddy banks as surely as flies flock to a bowl of clabber.

The kid didn't take much interest in the stuff they were trying to teach him over at the schoolhouse, but he soon learned that his big, red-covered *World History* book, when opened to the middle and held close to his chest, was perfect camouflage for the current issue of *Field and Stream* or *Sports Afield*. Countless study-hall hours were spent devouring adventures written by the likes of Jason Lucas, Ted Trueblood and Homer Circle. And it was among those well-read, dog-eared pages the Kid learned of an angling technique he would use to good advantage for the rest of his days.

The articles spoke of lunker bass, trophy wall-eye and hawg catfish, of the epic battles they would provide after being lured to the hook on a dark, moonless night, of the frogs and minnows, plentiful in the weedy shallows, and of the predators prowling among them in search of an easy meal. He learned of using a dark lure on a dark night, that an old moss-back will see its silhouette even against the blackest sky. And it was then that the plan was hatched.

"There's basketball practice tonight over to the schoolhouse," the kid fibbed that evening at supper. (He didn't mind bending the truth a little if it meant getting the chance to hook that great bass.) "An' I'll probably be a little late gettin' back 'cause we're practising for the big tourney." The old folks paid him no mind as he disappeared into the shadows and made straight for the shed to retrieve his rod and reel.

He usually carried his tackle, what little he had, in a rusty Prince Albert tobacco tin, but tonight he rummaged in the darkened shed for an old, seldom-used, black-painted Crazy Crawler. The kid's granddad had bought it on sale at the hardware store just about the time the Japanese delivered that suckerpunch to Pearl Harbor. They had tried it in the creek a few years back, but the sunfish and bullheads paid no attention to it. The kid had read in one of the magazine stories that the noisy, clattering topwater lure was just the ticket for fooling a smart old bass on a dark night, so maybe– just maybe . . .

Overcast and threatening rain, it was warm and humid as only the Hoosier hinterland can be, and as the kid stood quietly on the pond's muddy bank, he watched the wink of fireflies and the flickering glow of heat lightning playing on the western horizon. Spring peepers chirped from among the rushes, and the occasional booming challenge of a bullfrog blended with the low and ominous rumble of the approaching storm.

With a mighty two-handed cast, the kid sent the Crazy Crawler arcing high into the inky blackness. It landed somewhere on the still waters of the pond with a splash he was sure could be heard clear across the pasture to old man Tully's farmhouse. Just as he had read in the magazines, the kid slowly counted to 100, and after taking up the slack in the heavy, braided line, gave the plug a tentative twitch. A bubbling gurgle came from somewhere out of the night, and as he slowly cranked the handle of his ancient Bronson reel he could feel the darting wobble of the crawler.

The strike was unexpected coming so soon after his first cast: a vicious, smashing jolt that nearly wrenched the Gep from his hands. But the kid reacted instinctively, arching the heavy rod and setting the hooks deep in the jaws of the great bass. He could hear the rattle and splash as his unseen opponent tail-walked the dark surface of the pond in an effort to throw the plug. The spring-steel rod had all the sensitivity of a locust fence post, but the backbone of a mule, and soon the rod's relentless pressure and the kid's determination had the nearly spent smallmouth bass wallowing in the shallows.

The kid waded into the cool, ankle-deep water and by the glow of a brilliant lightning flash, pounced upon the she-bass and clutched her nearly seven pounds to his chest. It was then he was faced with the awful reality of his deed–he couldn't keep his wondrous prize. He couldn't take her home. He couldn't even tell anyone of his great conquest. Because if old man Tully ever got wise or if his folks found out, well, he was sure to be grounded for the rest of the year, or maybe the bike or even the .22 or . . .

Reluctantly his decision was made. He had to turn her loose. As he fumbled in the darkness to remove the hook from her jaw, she gave a mighty shake of her head, and the hook pulled free. She floundered briefly in the shallow water and then, with a thrust of her tail, disappeared into the dark and mysterious depths of the pond.

Only then did the kid feel the searing pain in his thumb where the treble hook had gashed his flesh to the bone as his trophy made her bid for freedom.

The rain had started to fall by the time the kid got back to the house. When his Pa asked why he was so muddy and what had happened to his thumb, the kid looked at the floor and mumbled something about taking the short cut from the schoolhouse and getting tangled up in some barbed wire. "sure you did," his Pa said knowingly. He poured some turpentine on the Kid's slashed thumb, and wrapping a strip of clean rag around it, allowed as how he would probably survive.

And now, after nearly a half-century, the kid still loves to pursue trophy smallmouth in the dark of the night. But you know, he never did get to tell anybody about that night when he caught the big bass in Tully's pond–until now . . .

How, you may wonder, after all those many years, do I know so much about that kid? Heck, that's easy. I still have that old steel rod and that black-painted Crazy Crawler. And someday I'll show you that ugly scar running down the side of my thumb!

Ron Miller is an award-winning outdoor writer, columnist and broadcaster, Past President and Life Member of the Outdoor Writers of Canada. He lives in Winnipeg, Manitoba.

HOW NOT TO CURE THE MUSKIE ITCH
By Bob Rife

I like catching a trophy fish as much as the next person. The thrill of setting the hook, playing the fish and then exhibiting a sizeable prize does something for the ego.

Admittedly when it comes to trophy fish, my problem has, on occasion, been that ego is spelled egg–served raw all over my face.

Recently I got the muskie itch. It was a combination of things.

First there was a call from Danny Wu, an angling companion, who is usually disguised as a Chinese restaurateur, but in mufti dashes about wearing an oddball white hat. He said Morley Wood had phoned from Port Severn to say that the muskies were really hitting.

Morley, a grizzled veteran, has been guiding members of the sporting fraternity on muskie hunts since he was 17 years old.

Queried about his age, Morley adroitly sidesteps saying, "My father, Anthony, guided until he was 86." If Morley's greying hair is brought into the conversation, he mumbles something about being "a little past 39," while insisting he neither owns nor plays badly on a violin.

But he knew an itching angler when I called asking how things were going. "You should see the picture of one I caught a week ago," he said. "A 34-pounder. It was 50 inches long. Got it on a Swim Whizz, a perch model."

Just what I'd always wanted to catch, a 30 pound-plus muskie. I wanted it so bad I ground my teeth. It was the ultimate Canadian trophy fish. This was my chance. I knew it. I just knew it.

I asked if, maybe, I could borrow that lucky lure, use it.

"Nope," he said. "That muskie bit right into the plug. One of its teeth put a hole in it. I didn't know 'til then that it was hollow, made of plastic. Now it fills full of water, doesn't work worth a darn. I might try to epoxy it, but, well . . ."

I thought of my own lures. "I've still got that Creek Chub Silver Flash that a muskie put marks on last year. You think it might work again?"

"Sure," Morley answered, setting the hook in his soon-to-be client. "Really, that's my favourite–the six-inch jointed model. Best lure for muskie in this area of Georgian Bay."

I could almost see him smile when I said, "We're on our way."

The Severn locks open at 8:30 a.m., and we were there in time to be the first boat through, first into the big bay. The sun searched between wind-twisted clouds, burning away morning mists and spotlighting autumn-touched trees on islands and headlands.

We rounded a channel buoy, and Morley urged us to rig our lines. "We'll work the edge of the reef. It's about 25 feet of water."

I attached the Silver Flash to a 20-inch length of 45-pound-test steel leader. I respect a muskie's chomping power.

About 10:15, with the wind picking up and quartering to the south-west, my rod bowed, and the big Penn reel started to sing.

I jumped to the rod, lifted it from the holder and felt the pumping, head-shaking first dive of a big muskie. "My trophy!" I yelled. "I knew it! My trophy!"

It was a humwangdinger of a battle–the charging monster crossed Danny's line, happily not before he was able to crank his lure in and out of trouble. It made dashing runs and then a tail-wagging leap I'll always remember.

Finally the huge fish rolled over on the surface in exhaustion.

I guided it carefully with my rod, bringing it to where Morley could reach in, haul it aboard. Oh, what a red-finned beauty!

"It's really hooked good," Morley shouted. "The lure's crossways in its mouth. A real nice fish. I'll have it in a moment–no problem."

Right. But you don't tempt fate with words like that when I'm fishing.

Sure enough. With a tremendous slap of its tail, the muskie jerked free from Morley and dived for the bottom. I lifted the rod high, higher, trying to put pressure on.

There was a lurch and a thwong that vibrated up the rod to my tight-gripped hands. The line went limp–the fish was gone.

Morley was stunned. "I don't believe it," he said again. "That's never happened to me before in all the years I've been fishing."

Chef Wu looked at the trophy-mangled leader and then at my face.

I put a hand to my cheek, feeling for egg.

Bob Rife is a freelance writer and photographer, and former Outdoors Editor of *The Globe and Mail* in Toronto. He lives in Scarborough, Ontario.

THE ICE-FISHING PENTATHLON
By Geoff Coleman

Ice fishing is not really considered a sport per se by most people. A recreation or hobby, yes, an excuse, definitely, but not a sport. Those people obviously do not know of the five events in the ice fisherman's pentathlon.

In sport, finishing a game in a tie is often compared to the experience of kissing your sister. In fishing, catching a fish through a hole in the ice must be about the same as planting one on your sibling. You may have caught a fish, but it probably didn't run too much, and it was likely hand-bombed to the surface as quickly as possible so you could put your mitts back on. And one thing is for sure, it didn't make any great leaps to throw the hook–unless you fish like Malcolm McDonald does.

On one of the many days he spends on the ice, Mac was jigging for whitefish. Like any good Scotsman, he was getting his money's worth from his licence using the allowable two holes. They were drilled about five feet apart, and he stood between them so he could work them both at the same time. He would raise one arm and then the other in a secret jigging motion like some kind of drunken semaphore flagman.

Apparently the fish were getting whatever message he was sending, because shortly Mac was into a good whitefish. Laying down the other rod, he brought the fish skilfully to the surface, all the while explaining that whiteys have a soft mouth, and the hook can come free at any second if you aren't careful.

With the fish right beneath the ice, Mac expertly turned its head and pulled it clear of the ice hole and into the air. At this point, however, he forgot all his wisdom about how a whitefish can come unpinned at any second. As we watched in disbelief, the fish spit the hook in mid-air and vaulted gracefully into the other hole with the precision entry of an Olympic diver.

If you were impressed by that basketball game promotion a few years ago when the guy "swished" the million-dollar shot from the opposite baseline, try to get a flopping whitefish to hit the hole from five feet.

In the first combined events of the pentathlon–basketball and diving–Mac had earned a tie but lost it in overtime.

Another sport that shows up in the competition is retriever trials. Mac probably wished he had a certain black Lab named Salty with him the day the whitefish did its Houdini imitation. This dog had earned a special spot in the Retriever's Hall of Fame when it left its comfortable bed in a Lake Simcoe fish hut to collar an escaping lake trout.

A two-foot by four-foot hole had been chainsawed through the ice inside the hut, and when a laker came unhooked about a foot from the surface, the dog dove through it after the fish. After a few anxious seconds, he managed to corral the laker and bring it back to the hole where he and the fish were hauled from the water. With Salty's tail in high gear and the trout flopping around at the other end, it was hard to tell which end of the dog was wagging most. The Lab enjoyed a special feed of trout that night.

Even that daring plunge cannot quite match the legendary pentathlon swims taken by an ice-fishing Finlander.

Veikko loved his sauna as much as he loved his ice fishing and his solitude. He was renowned for positioning his well-insulated ice hut far from the crowds, and stoking up the stove until the ice practically melted beneath his feet. Then he would strip down to his skivvies and jump in.

One day the arrival of a new hut was announced by a noisy chainsaw cutting out a big rectangle of ice, and it was much too close for the swimming Finn's liking. It was so close that a whitefish could have jumped from Veikko's hut to the other with a running start and a bit of a tailwind.

The Finlander had been doing really well for fish and didn't want to share the spoils with anyone; so when he took his last polar-bear plunge of the day in the gathering dark, he grabbed an extra breath of air and swam over to the neighbouring hut, surfacing in the hole like a cross between a Scandinavian submarine and Glenn Close in the bathtub scene from *Fatal Attraction*.

The reaction of the guys in the newly arrived hut was predictable, and that's when sprinting joined basketball, diving, retriever trials and swimming as the final event in the ice-fishing pentathlon.

Geoff Coleman is one of Ontario's top outdoor writers with credits in every major fishing magazine. When not fishing, writing or taking pictures, he is a high-school geography teacher in Fenelon Falls, Ontario.

FISHING LESSONS
By Marty Roberts

I really don't know when, or even how, it was formed, but the Shoot and Hook Outdoors Society was perhaps the most elite group of outdoorsmen that ever existed. When it first began, there were only six members, and only once in its history did the society ever admit another, bringing the total to seven. This is where I come in.

I was always aware of the Shoot and Hook Outdoors Society, although at the time I didn't know that they had a name, or for that matter, considered themselves a club. As a young teenager, I was always on the lookout for new places to fish and hunt. I knew that the six guys that always seemed to meet at ol' Doc Williams' clinic were constantly coming and going with either rod or gun in hand, and it was only natural to think that they knew what they were doing. Perhaps if I could hook up with them, I might find those secret places I had always heard of but never found.

It finally happened on the opener of trout season that spring. I started out two hours before sunrise, not necessarily to get a head start but to sneak past all those No Trespassing signs unnoticed. Catfish Creek ran for miles around town, but there was one stretch that had been posted for as long as I had known it. This particular year, I was going to find out why.

To get to this forbidden piece of water, I had to cut through the churchyard and then crouch my way along the hundred yards or so through the cemetery to the creek bank. I walked along the edge a little way and found a nice spot under a big old willow where I could set myself up for the day. It was perfect because no one could see me from any direction.

I waited until the sun was almost up and threw in a line. The worm was barely wet when I heard the ruckus from up in the graveyard. It seemed like an eternity but was probably only minutes before my heart slowed down to normal pace. It did, however, take a couple of hours for my skin to return to normal colour. The racket was coming from the half=dozen fishermen trying to sneak their way down to the creek. And who was in the lead but none other than Pastor Buck McElroy. It suddenly struck me that the reason for the No Trespassing signs wasn't because the church was sacred ground but because Pastor Buck was a leading member of the Shoot and Hook Club. Following close behind were Uncle Thornald and Cousin Jimmy. They weren't anybody's relatives but just preferred to be called by those titles. Next came Hal and Ernie, the old-timers of the group. At that time, I didn't even know their names but was well aware of their expertise in fishing. Bringing up the rear, with rod in one hand and jug of Ol' Porch Climber in the other, was Doc Williams. Doc was about the best physician anyone had ever known, but on the opener of any season you were best advised not to require his services.

I was just figuring out a way to scram out of there when my trusty and rusty steel rod doubled over. My choices were to throw the rod in and run like hell, or fight this prize to the end. As I wrestled with the lunker brookie, I forgot about the intruders and was deeply entranced with the task at hand. Once the fish tired out and I was bringing him up to the net, I glanced over my shoulder only to see six very angry men ready to pounce.

I knew of only one way out of this mess. I pulled out the hook from what was the largest brook trout of my life and threw the five-pound-plus fish back into the creek. I looked back at the intruders and said, "Nothin' but small ones here, fellas." I began to calmly pack up my gear.

Although I was anxious to get out of there, I couldn't resist looking back . . . only to see five of the men scrambling to get their lines in the water where I had released the monster. The sixth? Well, ol' Doc was resting up against a gravestone taking a big slug of Porch Climber when I last saw him.

That was my first meeting with the members of the Shoot and Hook Society, but before that fishing season ended, I was admitted into membership in the club. Not only that, I was unanimously elected chairman in charge of all chores. Bubbling with exuberance, but short on common sense, I accepted my new post. It was after I accepted that they told me the next election would be in 20 years.

Being the youngest and most recent addition to the club, I did not think it wise to be late for the next meeting, my first full meeting as a full-fledged member. Besides I had to supply the sandwiches, which I had already stored in Doc's operating room. All meetings were held at Doc's clinic. I found the temperature of the operating room was just right for partridge sandwiches and venison sausage. Doc also found it a convenient stash for his endless supply of Ol' Porch Climber. Besides, the antiseptic smell of his home-made brew didn't seem so out of place in there.

Doc was the only member of the club on hand when I got there, but gradually the other members arrived. Ernie and Hal, the two elderly brothers and my main mentors, came first. I heard their '34 Plymouth screech to a halt outside the clinic. That car had an unmistakable sound all its own. The four-door coach was fantastic for hunting trips because there was enough room in the thing to hold five or six hunters as well as a couple of dogs.

The senior siblings entered with their usual fanfare. Hardly a word was spoken although the odd grunt was audible. They stamped mud, at least I think it was mud, from their rubber boots and plunked themselves down in the two chairs nearest the pot-bellied stove. Without saying a word, Doc passed the jug, and Ernie took a long pull on it before passing it to Hal.

As this was going on, Uncle Thornald and Cousin Jimmy entered the room cussin' each other out a mile a minute. It seems that Jimmy was not impressed by driving to the meeting on his father's Massey-Ferguson.

"It's cold on the back of that thing," shouted Jimmy.

"Well, if you wouldna' run my truck into the outhouse we coulda' left the tractor at home," retorted Thornald.

The last to arrive was Pastor Buck McElroy. Buck was not like the rest of the boys. He was much more refined, and of this I was sure, slightly more educated. Buck quite often provided the stability that our club needed. One thing I have learned about old hunters is that they are very stubborn and love to argue at every opportunity. Pastor Buck somehow was able to keep peace during most of our gatherings.

Doc Williams banged a specimen bottle on the desk to bring the meeting to order, and then proceeded to fill the bottle with another couple of ounces of Ol' Porch Climber.

"What I want to propose," he said, "is that we take some of our club money and buy ol' Lefty MacPherson's little rowboat. Ever since Lefty lost that arm of his in the dynamite accident, he can't do nothin' but row in circles anyway. The way I figger it, we should be able to pick 'er up real cheap."

"Does a motor come with it?" asked Uncle Thornald.

"Nah," said Doc, "but we got the kid here to do our rowin'."

I hated being referred to as the kid. Just because I was the most-recent member of the club, and because the closest in age was Jimmy at 15 years my senior, I was the kid. It meant that whenever there was any physical labour to be done, it was automatically my job. It had now become my goal to be able to outwit these guys into doing their own work.

It was decided that Doc would do the negotiating with Lefty, and we would buy the boat provided that the price was within the budget of the club's funds. Doc wouldn't say exactly why but only that he was the best person to haggle with Lefty. He said Lefty owed him a favour from many years ago, and that it had something to do with several visits for penicillin shots.

A few days later, Doc had the boat on the roof of his car. I asked him how much it cost, and Doc really surprised me. He must have been one heck of a negotiator because Lefty outright gave it to us. I said that I felt we should have given him something for the boat, but apparently Lefty just wanted to forget the whole matter entirely.

It really was a nice old boat. It was sturdy and very well built. It was certainly heavy, as it took four of us to take it off Doc's car roof and carry it to the water. It was reasonably comfortable for four guys, and we usually took turns. It seems that I was always in the boat, though, manning the oars. In fact, by the end of the day, I was quite sick of that rotten old scow. I was soon planning for the hunting season when I could conveniently have an accident and blow a hole in the bottom of it.

The day on the water finally ended, and after putting the boat on the roof of the car, I melted into the back seat and watched the treetops go by as we headed for Doc's place. Everyone was pleased with the boat's performance. There were only a few complaints about the fact that the trolling speed could have been a bit faster. Personally, I was still planning how to rid myself of that awful, back-breaking monster.

I had just come up with five or six different plans when I felt the car take a sharp turn into Doc's driveway. I noticed that his garage door was wide open, and it struck me like a lightning bolt.

"Why don't we park this in the garage?" I said, "to keep someone from stealing it?"

Doc didn't answer, but he must have heard me because he just kept on driving right into the garage where we came to a rather abrupt halt with a very loud smash. Splinters of wood flew all over the place. Doc forgot that with the scow on the car roof it would be too high to get through the door.

Everyone piled out of the car and stared in disbelief at the remains of our club's beautiful, new boat. All was quiet, except for the muffled snickering that came from me. Doc picked up the paddle end of a broken oar and leered in my direction. I never looked back. I'm sure I set a new world record in the dash home to safety.

The other members seemed to have forgotten about the boat by the time we gathered for the next regular monthly meeting of the Shoot and Hook

Outdoors Society. We were all there in Doc's clinic. All of us except Doc, that is. He was still tied up in the back room with a patient. It seemed little Tommy Pefferlaw had split open his noggin in a fall from the old oak behind his house. His mother was also in the waiting room with the rest of us, and she seemed mighty anxious; I really don't know if it was because of little Tommy or because Cousin Jimmy kept staring at her and making rude comments about Doc conducting business when he should be starting the meeting.

The sewing task was soon finished, and Tommy and his mother were rushed out the door. Doc came into the room, still drying off his hands as he called the meeting to order. The minutes of the last meeting were read and passed, and we were now discussing new business.

The members were asked, one by one, and each time the answer was the same: "Nothin' this month." That is until we got to Pastor Buck.

"I've got something to say," boomed Buck in his best sermonesque voice.

I sensed that this meant he was serious because I had only ever heard that tone in his voice when he was giving a real rip-roarin' sermon. Usually on a real hot day, when the church windows are open, I can hear him from down at the creek. I often marvel at the coincidence of the best fishing hole being adjacent to the church cemetery.

"I move," said Buck, "that fishing on church property on Sunday mornings be banned for club members. Furthermore, I move that members of this Society attend church on a regular basis."

We were stunned. Uncle Thornald and Cousin Jimmy choked on the swigs of Ol' Porch Climber that they had just gulped down. Hal and Ernie started tapping their hearing aids on the table as though they were malfunctioning. Doc, well he just sat there staring at Buck as though his eyes would burn a hole right through him.

"Why in the world would you propose something like that?" Doc asked. "You know as well as the rest of us that Sunday morning is the best time to cast a line on Catfish Creek. All the other fishermen in town are in church at that time."

"Well, for starters, every time you guys get a fish on, you whoop and holler so loud that it disturbs my service," replied the pastor. "Secondly, the language you use when you lose one puts half the congregation into shock. And finally, your wives aren't too pleased either, making them sit alone in church every week. Besides, they made me promise that if I couldn't get you guys off the creek on Sunday mornings I'd have to put up No Trespassing signs again.

The motion before us was argued well into the late hours of the evening. The discussions got hot and heavy, and we were down to our last jug of Ol' Porch Climber. Finally Buck won out, and we all decided that there was no other choice but to go along with him. Besides, the married members of the group knew that they would lose the argument at home anyway.

The next Sunday morning was an event to be remembered. There at the back of the church sat the entire membership of the Shoot and Hook Outdoors Society, all decked out in their best suits. Unfortunately Pastor Buck was not to see it. An announcement was made that he was ill that morning and his assistant would be conducting the service that day. The proceedings were soon over, and we only had to wake Doc twice during the sermon.

As the congregation left the building, we all rushed for our cars, slipped off our suit coats, and put on waders and vests. Rods were at the ready as we collectively rushed through the cemetery for the creek.

We all hit the crest of the knoll that stretches along the creek, at the same time. We stopped in our tracks in unison as well. There sat Pastor Buck, leaning up against the big old willow, drawing on a big cigar. He was wet to the waist, and there were four nice brook trout at his side.

"Whatever kept ya, boys?" he whispered. "The fishin's been great."

Marty Roberts is a freelance writer and active member of the Outdoor Writers of Canada. He lives in Fort Erie, Ontario.

THE ONE THAT GOT AWAY
by Michael Snook

In a sport that spins more unlikely yarns than any other, there's one particular kind of tale that outdoes them all. In fact, there are so many of these stories–of the one that gets away–that it would take almost every angler in the world to tell them all. Make that every angler.

It's always the biggest, longest, rarest fish of all–the trophy that nobody gets a glimpse of, except you, the one who catches it. It's yours only for the briefest of moments, and only you live to tell the tale. If even a fraction of these stories are to be believed, then the world's lakes and rivers are filled to overflowing with the most magnificent fish ever known.

Here is such a fish. And such a story. It dates from a time around my 12th birthday, sometime during the last millennium. Close to my family home was a rock point that jutted well out into a northern lake. Everyone should have such a point nearby, and every fishing story should have just such a classic setting. I didn't know it then, of course, but I'd be leaving this in the near future. At age 12, I still took it all completely and gloriously for granted. All the civilized wonders of the modern world, all its appetites, were just around the corner, just out of sight. For me, there was only the lake and the fish in it.

Each day after school, I'd walk out to the point, just a half-mile or so around the bay from my front door, and go fishing. I owned an old fibreglass rod, an early model open-face spinning reel, and a handful of spoons to tie on and cast from shore. Fishing like this, only a few weeks after the ice-out, I could always count on catching lots of small wall-eye. We called them pickerel then, though they weren't. The nearest pickerel was actually more than a 1000-miles south, enjoying a much finer climate and far less fishing pressure.

The technique for harassing the spring wall-eye of my youth was simple enough. Cast out a spoon, retrieve it near bottom, just tickle the tops of the rocks. Wait for that touch that somehow said "fish," not "rock," and set the hook.

Guess right and catch enough fish for dinner, almost any day of the week, right up until the water got warm enough for a real, all-day swim.

Guess wrong and lose a lure that cost a week's allowance. We regulars at the point would, of course, never lose a lure. We would carefully mark the location of those that were. Later in the warm June sunshine, we would dive on the rocks and stock up for the season with what we found. It was a matter of pride for us that we did not buy our lures. Not ever.

We never caught anything of any size. The occasional three or four-pound pike would drive youthful adrenalin levels to new and ecstatic heights, but the catch of the day was usually a few pan-sized wall-eye averaging around a pound each. There was, however, for a young angler still new to this most hopeful of sports, always the chance, the dream, the possibility, of something really big clamping on to that old red-and-white spoon.

There was a day late in the spring when the land was trying its best to return to winter. The sky was slate grey, the temperature just above freezing, and the wind tore in out of the north-west. Not a good day for wall-eye. They don't like this kind of weather, and I'm not that fond of it myself. To catch any fish at all, I'd have to keep my balance on rocks covered with frozen spray, face straight into an icy blow and breathe the life back into insensate fingers every few minutes. It would be another perfect day to go fishing.

For several hours, I cast and retrieved, cast and retrieved. Hoped. Cast some more. On days like this, true anglers are born. Fools that will stay out in any weather, we know that the very next cast, for certain sure, will bring a fish. And if not that one, then the next, or the next. Such true anglers begin each cast with wild enthusiasm. As the retrieve progresses and no fish are found, we sink into a fatalistic hole. We know we have no business doing what we're doing, that it's an utterly hopeless task we've set for ourselves–as cast after cast ends fishless. But each next cast is another matter entirely. It is a new dawn, a new era, the essence of hope itself. The next cast is the very heart of the mystery of fishing. Every angler knows, as a matter of faith, that the next cast will be *the* cast. And ultimately, it is.

And so I cast and cast again. Youth possesses limitless energy. Finally there was a pull on the line. I pulled back and snagged my best spoon on a rock.

Now as I've said, it was a matter of pride for me never to lose a spoon to those rocks. I could always feel it, just when I was getting in a little too deep, give the rod a little jerk, speed up the retrieve just a hair and stay away from the rocks. But on this particularly cold and nasty day, with no fish biting, I'd lost my edge, my concentration had gone. I'd snagged. How lucky I felt that no one was there to see my shame. I had a reputation to protect.

Well, at least I would get my lure unstuck. I pulled and heaved, walked down the rocks a way, pulled some more. I walked back the other way, pulled some more–and then it moved. Slowly, steadily, it moved. Out into the lake.

It was as if the entire bottom of the lake had started to slide away from me, ever so gently but very firmly. If you had asked me then if the earth moved, I would have answered, "yes."

And it kept moving, in the opposite direction from where I wished it would go. I was spooled up with twelve-pound-test line, and my reel filled with a good 200 yards of it. I was going to fight whatever had my lure, haul it in and get a good look at it.

Except nothing I did could change its mind about where it–whatever *it* was–was going. Straight out into the lake with complete determination. The line just stripped off my reel. Steadily, inexorably, I tightened up the drag as much as I dared. No effect. I pulled back until the rod was bent double. No result.

Now you have to understand, there was no frantic action here, no panic. In fact, it was all happening at a very leisurely pace. Inevitably, but leisurely. The creature that had my lure in its jaws was not in any hurry. It was going somewhere but it had all day to get there. Maybe even all year. It was almost as if it had no awareness of my presence at all, of my lure in the corner of its mouth or the slender monofilament that connected us to each other.

It was certainly not paying any attention to anything I was doing.

It crossed my mind that this was a very, very, very large fish. I began to get quite enthusiastic about it and how, once I landed it, I would get a picture of the two of us and they'd probably run it in the local paper. After all they ran pictures of fishermen with big fish all summer, and this was certainly going to be a big fish.

I was quickly running out of line. Maybe there were 20 yards left on the spool. There was no stopping this creature. I began to despair. I would lose this fish without a real fight. He would slowly but surely take all my line off the spool, and I wouldn't even get to see him. This struck me as profoundly unfair.

Right about then I felt a subtle change–the rod felt different in my hands, and I looked out onto the lake. There was a boil on the surface of the water, quite a way off shore.

Something large came up to the surface, something that rolled over once then submerged with all the confidence of a sounding whale. I saw the white of its belly, immense and pale against the slate grey of sky and water.

The line on my spool reached its end. It snapped off with a tiny, anticlimactic "ping." The fish never even noticed.

My father and his friends told me later there were very big sturgeon in the lake, up to a hundred pounds. They said I probably snagged one, and he just swam away with my line and lure, never knowing they were there. I don't think so. I think I caught one and it got away. I think it came up once and rolled so I could see it. Fishermen are optimists, no matter what their age and experience. Without these characteristics they may not, could not, be fishermen.

A few years after this, I moved to the bright lights and the big city to the south. Back home the developers moved in, put pressure on my family and all the others along the beach, and bought them out. They planned to put in expensive condominiums. Progress, they said, would be better for everyone. They went broke before they built a thing, their line of credit running somewhat shy of their ambitions.

Sometimes the big ones get away.

Michael Snook is a freelance writer and television and radio producer based in Regina, Saskatchewan. He is the creator and producer of the television program *What on Earth* and outdoors columnist for the Regina *Leader Post* and Regina *Sun*.

ON PAST FAVOURS
By Wayne Curtis

The community was one of scattered wilderness farms, all of which bordered the river. Each one was apart from the other and had its own personality, the spirit of its owner. These farms were united as a community largely through bonds of respect for the other person's property and his or her welfare. In a transaction with a neighbour, the nod of a head was as good as a signature. Philosophies were exchanged over fence lines at haying time. Imaginations were nourished by loneliness, and each one's strongest characteristics were developed from exposure to him or herself alone. Indeed, there were characters here in Moores Siding, and as a youngster, I knew them all.

There was old Tom Wills who walked at night, talking to himself in a variety of tones and answering in imaginative voices, so that if you didn't know him and you heard him coming in the dark, you'd swear it was a crowd of men. Then there was old Charlie Eighton from the next farm. Chuck was a confirmed salmon poacher. Folks said it wasn't so much that old man Eighton wanted the fish he caught, but that he got his kicks from the risk of being caught sweeping a pool. For excitement he would poach in broad daylight. It was in his blood.

The fish wardens in those days were Ed Black and Raymond Mills. Old Ed was obsessed with his responsibility. "I'm sworn to protect the Atlantic salmon," he would say. "A dangerous species." He would help keep the balance in nature by saving the salmon link in life's chain, thus preserving mankind from extinction. It was said that Ed and Raymond would chase a poacher through the gates of Hell. All of us at Moores Siding had great respect for the wardens.

In the mid 1950s, the fish wardens travelled the river by canoe, and they became accustomed to long river runs of two or three days at a time, not an easy life. It was common to see them pitch a tent on the river bank near our farm and spend the night there. I can recall watching from the hilltop and catching the fragrance of salmon fillets sizzling on their campfire which snapped by the lee side of a canoe propped among the bushes. While Ray and Ed were from some 30 miles up the river, they soon became close friends of my father as they sometimes used our interval for a tenting area.

One autumn evening, after the salmon-angling season was closed for the year, the wardens made camp on the flats as they always did—only this night, Father invited the two men to our farmhouse to share the evening meal with the family. Ed and Ray were treated with heels of rum and the last drop of Scotch whisky in 20 miles. Voices loudened as they talked and laughed with Father, all cronies now in the old dining room.

Ed was telling Father of giving chase to an awkward poacher that same afternoon. "Yes," said Ed, "He was drifting with a long net, right through the salmon hole, just up around the bend from here . . . and in daytime! The gall of it!" He went on to tell Father of the man scrambling to get away, running up the steep river bank with the wet salmon net dragging on the grass, a couple of large salmon becoming entangled.

"He ran into a poplar treetop, left there by beaver," Ed continued. "His net caught up in the branches, and he had to leave it with a large salmon meshed, dead. But the son of a whore got away with one, or maybe two, large salmon."

He told us the poacher threw rocks from the hilltop, trying to hit them while they were untangling the net from the tree branches and putting it into their canoe. Ed then proceeded to lecture all of us on the dreadful condition of the resource, the amount of poaching that was going on and the trash that hung around the river in these parts, and how poaching would affect us all someday.

There was a rap on the kitchen door, and without waiting for an answer, Charlie Eighton entered the house. Charlie was in a fresh change of clothes, sporting his new plaid Mackinaw and his best felt dress hat. Under his arm, he was carrying a large salmon of about 20 pounds. He was probably repaying Father for a past favour, or maybe it was just a gift to a loyal neighbour. In any case, the salmon was completely wrapped in newspapers from its head to beyond its tail. Charlie walked up to the dining-room table where the men were grouped, the fish tucked neatly under his arm.

When he saw the two uniformed wardens sitting at the table, he said, "Here, Jack. Here's the rifle I borrowed from you last week."

He passed the long salmon nervously across the table to Father.

"Indeed!" said Father, and at once took the newspaper-wrapped fish across the dining room and stood it in the corner. Then he came back to the table and went on with his evening meal.

When Charlie was gone, the old warden was quick to remark, "Now that's my cut of a man."

Wayne Curtis is a freelance writer and author of *Currents in the Stream*, *One Indian Summer*, *Fishing the Miramichi* and *The Growing Seasons*. He lives in Newcastle, New Brunswick.

ONLY WHEN YOU WANT ONE ♦ ♦ ♦

By David E. Scott

The man at the tackle shop near the Bahia Mar was enthusiastic about what could be caught in the murky waters of the canal running past the vacation house I had rented in Fort Lauderdale.

Red snapper, tarpon, grouper and even the occasional sand shark, he said, laying out all the equipment I'd need. He recommended frozen shrimp as bait, and just happened to have a freezer full. Bait shrimp must be specially treated because Harry's bait shrimp cost more than the jumbo ones in the supermarket.

Something hit my bait moments after it sank in the filthy water. Up came a yellowish creature seven or eight inches long, covered with spikes and spines. It flopped around on the lawn growing larger by the minute like an inflating balloon until it was almost perfectly round except for the tail sticking out. The hook was out of sight down its throat–behind two front teeth almost as large as mine. I cut the leader and tied on another hook.

Soon there was a tug at the line, and when I set the hook, whatever it was made a run across the canal. The fish put up a fun fight for its size–about two pounds. It, too, had swallowed the hook so I couldn't release it either. It lay on the lawn, a brilliant bluish silver, dulling rapidly to grey.

I resumed fishing, waiting for that red snapper to hit. Behind me I heard a pig grunting, but the only things in sight were those two weird fish and the small table supporting my dark rum and soda. I went back to examine the fish. The spiky balloonfish, later identified as a blowfish, was still puffing and threatening to come apart at the seams. The other, now a dull grey, lay on its stomach glaring at me and grunting like a pig. It kept this up for 15 minutes before expiring. This specimen was later identified as a grunt. It makes the noise by grinding pharyngeal teeth in its throat.

The next specimen out of the canal was built like a perch and had vivid striping. It was hooked in the lip and had nothing to say, so I gently removed the hook and returned it to the canal.

Something was nibbling the bait, but whenever I struck, the hook was bare. I raised the line slowly and the nibbling continued. Then, whatever it was took hold, and I pulled up an enormous crab whose shell was seven inches in diameter and a vivid metallic blue. Even its fat, armoured legs were bright blue.

I was relieved when this creature let go of the hook and scuttled surprisingly quickly and with unerring aim straight back to the canal, sideways, of course.

I got three more blue crabs that afternoon, three blowfish–each of which inhaled the hook–and four grunts.

At dinner that evening, a local couple kindly identified the various fish. "But what did you do with the crabs?" Mike asked excitedly.

"Let them go."

"Oh no, you didn't?" he exploded, incredulous. "Those are the greatest delicacy available in the state. Some people spend a whole day fishing in the hopes of catching just one–and you threw *four* back, . . . " his voice trailed off as though he'd realized there was no point discussing the matter with such an abysmal idiot.

I fished every afternoon for the next five days before catching another crab. Lots of blowfish–at one hook each, I was now on first-name terms with Harry at the bait shop–lots of those stripey little jobs and several species of grunt. But no blue crabs, not even green, brown, yellow or red ones.

Late on the fifth day, up came granddaddy blue crab, and he didn't get away. He crawled out of a big bucket and a cardboard carton, but he couldn't escape the bathtub.

We were having Maine lobster that night, and my crab went into the pot after they were cooked. The rest of the family was revolted at the thought of eating anything that could survive in the sewage of that canal.

Just as well. That metallic blue crab was the most delicious meal I'd had in years. I didn't even bother with my lobster.

The crab didn't taste fishy. It had a flavour best described as nutty and was exquisite.

There were none of those crabs for sale in any of the fish shops I tried the next day, and though I spent my last three days in Fort Lauderdale desperately trying to catch another, it was not to be. Word of the tourist's contract on blue crabs must have leaked out to the denizens of the canal.

David E. Scott is the author of five guidebooks to Ontario and editor of this anthology. He lives in Ailsa Craig, Ontario.

THE CATASTROPHE BASS
By Ron Miller

The strike was not unexpected. Still it came as a nerve-tingling surprise; that almost-electric moment when you feel the vital energy of a good fish transmitted from the mysterious depths through the slender graphite wand to the very core of your being. The husky she-bass stayed unusually deep for this time of year. During the last days of May, north-west Ontario's Catastrophe Lake can provide smallmouth-bass fishing to rival the most tail-walking, spray-flinging action to be found anywhere. However, this old girl preferred to fight her battle amid the rock and rubble of the six to eight-foot depths.

The first bassing expedition of the season is usually filled with that marvellous sense of not knowing what is going to happen next, and this adventure was not to be the exception. Shedding the confines of the bustling Winnipeg metropolis, we had journeyed to this unsullied bit of nature, conveniently hidden only a short distance off Highway 596, hurriedly launched our boat and wasted no time seeking the rocky and relatively shallow, wind-chopped points.

Experience gained in seasons past assured us the bass would be on or near the quickly warming, boulder-strewn shelves and would eagerly accept our quarter-ounce chartreuse jig and twister-tail offerings.

The contest waxed and waned in true story-book fashion until the smallie could be seen alongside the boat in the somewhat murky two to three-foot depths. Her sizzling runs and head-shaking determination proved once again that, ounce for ounce and pound for pound, the smallmouth bass is the hardest-fighting fish in fresh water. Gently lipping her hefty three pounds into the boat and removing the barbless aggravation in her jaw, she was quickly returned to the water to tend to her business on the spawning beds.

The following two days of this angling odyssey proved just as rewarding and action filled as the opening moments, although for my part, tinged with just a wee bit of disappointment. You see, in the jumble and confusion of my office where most of these fond memories are set to paper, there is, among the clutter of books, magazines and outdoor paraphernalia, a blank and unadorned vacancy on the wall directly above my desk; a place reserved for that one bragging-sized bass I have yet to land. Faced with the tyranny of old age, I find I hunger for a tangible representation of all the bass, both large and small, that have made life a rich and rewarding experience.

Coming across a long-forgotten, faded and dog-eared photograph helped recall a time many seasons past when that vacancy was very nearly filled. The photo, a nostalgic reminder of gentler times, brings back the heady essence of river bank gumbo, the smells of wet cedar and tar, my son Steve sitting on the sturdy, contoured fender of our '47 Chevy and chiding me for not being able to catch a fish for our supper. We had intended to spend a few idle moments on that sun-dappled summer afternoon casting into the slowly flowing waters of the Tippecanoe River, yet not really expecting to catch anything.

The spring steel Gep casting rod sent the heavy, nickel-plated Pflueger Limper arching high into a cloudless sky to land with a loud plop in mid-stream. Instantly a vicious strike drew the braided twenty-pound-test line fiddle-string tight, and after a few scorching runs, the fish jumped, tail-walking with blood-red gills flaring, and lord o' mercy, it was a smallmouth! Seven or eight pounds if it was an ounce! Not close to the eleven-pound monster that held the world record in 1955 but still the biggest bronzeback that had ever been seen in that neck of the woods.

One more cartwheeling jump, and the bright silver spoon, its single, brittle hook broken, arrowed over our heads to land in the bank-side brush. Frustration and disappointment ruled. Off came the battered, old fishing hat to be violently slammed to the tar-splattered dock and receive a good stomping! And that five-year-old whelp, sitting on the fender of the Chevy, howled with glee to see his old man do a clog dance on his hat!

That fond interlude was maybe 100,000 casts ago (and that same scrawny kid now pats me on the head and calls me little daddy), but never since has there been a bass of such grand proportions to set my heart a-pounding.

And now, on a hazy mid-July afternoon, with the sun suspended like a worn loonie in an azure sky, hope springs eternal. Catastrophe Lake (and I don't want to even speculate on how this lovely bit of Eden received its ominous-sounding name) just may offer the chance to fill that void over my desk.

I'm not overly ambitious. I don't yearn for the recognition, the status or, for that matter, the hassle that goes with holding a world record. A chunky three-and-a-half or four-pounder to grace my wall would happily put an end to the quest of nearly half a century.

In sympathy with the seasons, the technique for taking summer Catastrophe bass varies greatly from that of spring. There is a reef, or more correctly a plateau, smack-dab in the centre of the lake. Rising from the 60-foot depths, its flat, rubble-strewn top is aswarm with good bass. Slipping the point of a number one True Turn hook under the dorsal fin of a lively, four-inch red-fin chub, I committed the bottom-walking, Lindy-rigged outfit to the deep. The soft breeze and gentle chop made the drift just right, and I could feel the half-ounce sinker dancing among the rock and rubble thirty feet below. The pick up was almost imperceptible. Not bass-like at all; merely a heavy feeling to the rod. But at the moment of hook-set, all hell broke loose in that cool, shadowy world beneath the boat.

Fighting doggedly the fish stayed deep, reluctant to give up the sanctuary of the plateau. "A nice, eating-size northern," I thought aloud, for there have been some dandy pike in the twelve to fifteen-pound class taken off this reef. But no, racing for the surface on an almost-slack line, the fight became more bassy by the moment. And then in a mighty surge of sparkling spray, the great bass exploded the surface, tail-walking and pirouetting in her aquatic ballet. Give a little, take a little, a powerful surge to the depths, a blistering slash on the surface– and in a twinkling, the picture of that sleek, bronzed battler was permanently etched deep in the secret place in my mind where I like to store all the good stuff of life, and I thought: "Isn't this really what fishing is all about?"

Later that evening, after having dined royally on a couple of feisty one-pounders that were persuaded to stay for dinner, I took a stroll down to the dock for just one more look at my prize trophy finning quietly in the boat's live well. But something was wrong; a strange uneasiness and a line from an old song, something about being "vaguely discontented," kept flitting through my mind. A decision most surely had to be made. Having survived many years of peril, this noble creature deserved better than to become a dust catcher over my desk.

Motivated by the desire to have Steve's grandchildren–and indeed his great-grandchildren–enjoy the wholesome and exhilarating pleasure of playing a fine smallmouth on light tackle, and the knowledge that one less trophy on the wall can mean hundreds more in the lake, the decision was easy.

As the purple shadows of night stole softly over the western sky, I lifted the grand old girl from the live well and tenderly lowered her into the calm waters of the bay. For a brief but hopefully understanding moment, we were eye to eye; then with a single thrust of her mighty tail, she was gone.

Somewhere in the deepening twilight, a loon sang its haunting evensong; tonight, sleep would come gentle and untroubled . . .

Ron Miller is an award-winning, outdoor writer, columnist and broadcaster, Past President and Life Member of the Outdoor Writers of Canada. He lives in Winnipeg, Manitoba.

MOOSEHEAD 'N' THE SKUNK
By Herb M. Curtis

Now, I ain't much good at story tellin', as far as I know, like, and to tell the truth, I never knowed I had a story to tell 'til the day afore yesterday . . . that bein' the fourth day of August and a real hot one. I mind Mom sayin' to me. "Boys, she's hot!"

And me answerin', "Yep, she's downright Celcius all right, Mum dear!" Mom's me mother and a nice enough lady, most of the time . . . so long's ya don't cross her . . . somethin' like meself, I mean. I ain't no Yvon Durrel, but I kin handle meself in a small town.

Anyway, I was down by the river where it's cool, and me and Ben Miller was tryin' to make a still. I had Ben with me, cuz he's sort of an expert on liquor, bein' drunk most of the time like meself. It didn't matter, though. We didn't know diddly-squat about makin' liquor. I mean, you kin be drunk all yer life and still not know how to make the stuff. Oh, we had us a coil of copper pipe runnin' from a milk can just like we figured would work. We filled the can full o' potato peelings and sugar, and I forget what all, and built a fire under the can. She dripped all right, and we drank it almost as fast as she dripped, but I think all we had was potato juice, cuz that's what it tasted like, and it had no kick to it . . . and it don't matter none, anyway, cuz it don't have a thing more to do with the story than the fact that it was a hot day, and we ended up drier than a corn-meal fart and needin' a drink more than ever. She was real hot out, ya see, and we had this fire on and . . . well, anyway, while we was there, we noticed that the salmon was jumpin' like the devil across the river at the mouth of MacKenzie Brook. Salmon are always at the mouth of MacKenzie Brook on a hot day. They like cold water, ya see, and MacKenzie Brook is always just a little bit colder than the main river, so the salmon lay in there, kind o' half asleep like. Anyway, they were coming in and jumpin' like the devil just like I said before.

So Ben says to me, he says, "If we's only had a nit, we could fill 'er right there no trouble, eh?"

I speak right up and says, "You're right there, Ben old dog, but where in hell we gonna get a nit?"

"I don't know," he says.

Well, we set ourselves right down there on the sprills on the sidehill and begun to think. I always knowed I was the smartest one o' the two, and I proved it right then and there, fer I was the first one to think o' somethin'. I minded an old gaspereaux nit that Papa used to set fer gaspereaux and sea trout before he died 10 years ago, so I tolt Ben of it.

Well, sir, he figured it'd be a good outfit and all that, but he said he knowed of a better rig, an old tideway nit that'd reach damn near halfway 'cross the river, which is no slouch of a distance. He said it had a six-inch mash, and it belonged to his Uncle Henry, and he figured we'd ketch a pile o' fish in 'er, if Henry would lend it to us for a while–maybe for the price of a piece o' fish.

I asked 'im if he thought it'd be rotten, and he said "No," so we went and asked Henry for it, just like that.

Henry said he thought the old nit was rotten, but Ben stuck to his guns and said, "No, it weren't," and even if it was a bit rotten we'd be bound to pick up a few, anyway. So, we took it and strung 'er out down beside Henry's potato field, which was on the flat in front of Henry's house, just over the hill, like.

The nit was rotten all right, but we said we'd use 'er anyway and left 'er there on the grass with all the good intentions of picking 'er up later that night.

Well, about this time was supper time, so we went home and et. After supper, I and Ben said we should go girlin' for a little while before we go fishin' with the nit, but I only laughed cuz I knowed there weren't no girls around, and I knowed deep down that I were too homely to get the women anyway. But Ben now, he said he knowed of a couple o' women that was spendin' their holidays at Ned Porter's place, so we greased our hair right back and struck 'er for Ned's.

I asked Ben if he knowed them good 'nough to speak to, and he said he did, for he'd walked one of them home from Howard's which is about a five-mile walk and no slouch of a walk, either, if you're walkin', let's say, all alone with a little lady.

I asked Ben what 'er name was and if he was in love wit' 'er, and he said "Becky" and "No," but he said that he kissed 'er twice, once at Trissy Holden's and agin two miles further up the road . . . that would be right along there by the broken down-popple.

Well, Ned Porter was a bootlegger, and when we got there we found the girls had went home to wherever it was they was from.

"Good racket!" I said.

"Don't matter," said Ben. "Them girls wouldn't've looked sideways at a lad like you, anyway. I just thought that maybe you'd like to size them up a bit." Good old Ben was just thinkin' of me, you understand? He wanted me to see the girls.

So anyway, we had to have a little chat wit' Ned, so we sot right down and struck 'er talkin' about the weather, floods, scabby potatoes and stuff like that, not lettin' Ned know fer a minute that we was disappointed about no women on the scene. Old Ned, besides bein' a bootlegger, worked for the gov'ment on the road and never did nothin' and never had a castle on his hands in his life. Hands, look o' here, just like a school ma'ams. And he had money, too! Lots of 'er! Like that night, for example, we give 'im every cent we had before we left . . . sort o' traded in our money for two pints o' rye and a case o' Moosehead beer. We hadn't planned to get drunk, . . . well, not *real* drunk, anyway. But you know how it is, we was blue cuz there weren't no women to look at, and drinkin' was sort o' what seemed right, and you know how it is.

After a while, we struck 'er for Henry's, us about half cut, kind o' cross leggin' 'er, . . . the moon comin' up over Taylor's Mountain, which ain't really a mountain, and that bird that flutters his wings 'way up in the sky and no one kin ever see 'im . . . makin' that lonesome noise of his . . . Bill Layton was playin' his 'cordian and singin,' "I shot a sparrow wit' my bow 'n' arrow and 'twas I who kilt the cock robin . . . "

Old Bill couldn't sing to save his soul, but would do it at the drop of a hat, if ya know what I mean, and once he got started, you almost had to shove a potato in his throat to get him to shut up. Was a real pretty night with the toads singin' and the frogs fartin' right along with old Bill.

It was about 11 o'clock when we finally decided to go fishin', and we was just passin' Henry's house on our way to get the nit when we got a whiff of a skunk. Now, you know yerself what a skunk smells like! Anyway, the closer we got to the nit, the worse the smelt, and I guessed right then and there what'd happened. I figured a skunk had got 'imself caught in the nit, and by God, I was right, for there was one in it all right, and it was all tangled up and still alive, too.

"Good racket!" I said.

Well, we was in one hell of a scrape, for I didn't know what to do or nothin' else. Oh, but Ben knowed! Ben, who had drunk most of the rye and half the beer, he knowed!

Ben swung to me and said, "Don't you worry, buddybuddy pal, I know how to handle a skunk. No skunk kin piss on ya once you get 'im by the hind legs."

"Yeah," I said. "Well, you go right at 'er, Ben old dog. If ya don't mind, I'll just stand back here and have meself a quart o' beer. Go to 'er!"

Well sir, I watched and kept me distance, and I ain't lyin' one bit when I say that there stink'd knock ya down! 'Twas horrible! I had to laugh, though, watchin' Ben sneakin' up on that skunk, tryin' to get 'im by the tail. I told 'im that I would sooner pass the hand on old Annie Bert than grab that skunk, but he didn't say nothin', just kept sneakin'.

The skunk was all nervous 'n' everything and was all tangled 'n' everything, but Ben almost made it. Almost. With one hand in front of his face to protect him and his other hand about four inches from that skunk's tail, Ben almost didn't get sprayed.

What happened was, just as he grabbed for the tail, the poor old skunk flew off the handle and spewed poor Ben. And the stink would knock ya down!

"Good racket!" says I. "Now what?"

Ben didn't seem to hear me. He was doused, and it was too late to do anything about it. He was figurin' he might as well finish the job.

He did, too!

He freed the skunk, carried it a hundred feet away from the nit and sot it down nice and easy like, then went back to the nit.

And God, what a stink!

"So, what now?" I asked.

"We overhaul the nit," he says.

"What? How kin ya stand the smell o' yerself?"

"I'm too close to it," he says. "I don't smell a thing."

"Well, if you can't smell it, you must be dead from the arse up," I said, "for I can smell ya and I'm 20 feet away!"

"Can't smell a thing," he said. "Now give me a hand untanglin' the nit. We got fishin' to do!"

So I tolerated the stink the best I could and helped 'im untangle the nit, stopping only two or three times for a drink o' beer. When that was done, we overhauled the nit one more time into the boat, then drunk another quart o' beer while we figured out what we'd do next. Ben figured that the nit was too deep for the shaller water, so I being the one that didn't smell any worse than usual, went back up to Henry's and borried a flashlight. We figured that with a light, we'd be able to see the rocks and sticks and stuff on the bottom of the river.

I asked Henry for the light. He thought that a light was a pretty stupid thing for a couple o' poachers to use, cuz the wardens would be able to see us, but I told 'im that Ben said he wanted it, cuz the nit was so long and deep. Henry jist grinned and gave me the flashlight without a further aye, yes or no. "Good luck," was all he said.

So I sauntered back down to the river with the light. Me and Ben had one more beer and shoved off. I poled, and Ben stood in the front of the canoe. He'd elected himself as the lad what would throw the nit. He also got to hold the flashlight. That was Ben for ya! Always the big shot!

When we got into the current pretty good, Ben started throwin' the nit, kersplash, kersplash, kersplash, into the river, while I poled cross the current as fast as I could. That big long tideway nit strung out like beads across the river behind us, the prettiest thing you ever laid your eyes on.

"Hello! Can't throw a nit, kin I!" boasted Ben, and I had to admit that he'd done a real good job.

We drifted along at a pretty good clip, and I knowed that things seemed to be goin' too good. And, by God, I was right. Nothin' had ever worked that slick for us before, and it wasn't about to happen that slick for us now, either. I mean, we had screwed up makin' the still on that very day, so we might have known that this fishin' with a nit stuff wouldn't work any better.

What happened was, the nit, which was strung out clean across the river, fetched up on a big rock at the very end. The next thing ya know, we were hangin' by the nit on the current, a hundred yards or more downstream from the rock. The canoe hung sideways on the current makin' the awfulest noise ya ever heard in all yer life, . . . like about 40 lads all holdin' their paddles in the water. We hung there for about a minute or two until the nit tore–thank God she was rotten–and we was free. However, I think we left a good chunk of the nit hangin' from the rock.

Well, that was all right.

We sailed on for what must have been another whole two or three seconds, when the near end of the nit got caught up, and we was in another scrape. This time the rock was right underneath us. Ben lit the flashlight, and we sized up this second little darlin'. I could see that there was only about a foot o' water in this particular place, so I jumped in and freed the nit, jumped back in the canoe and poled it around to the other end of the nit. Ben grabbed the other end, and we were sailin' once agin. This time we sailed for a whole hundred yards before she caught up on another big rock about the size of a Volkswagen, and then we were in a *real* bad mood.

We sort o' lost control, if ya know what I mean.

I grabbed the bottom line o' the nit and Ben grabbed the top line, and we begun to give 'er hell, like the devil was after us, overhanding everything, rippin', tearin', Ben and me both swearin' every good oath we could think of. The nit corks and leads were beatin' on the side o' the canoe and makin' an awful racket, and wit' us swearin' like the devil and the flashlight on, I reckoned if a warden didn't ketch us, he'd have to be dead.

Well, ya'll never guess what happened!

Well sir, we just got the nit into the boat when the wardens *did* show up, turned their big lights on us, lit up the whole river and pretty near scared the poop out o' us.

"Let's make a run for it!" I said.

"Stay where you are," said Ben.

"You're crazy," I said. "We might be able to get away!"

"Don't worry, Bert me boy," said Ben the loon. "Them wardens ain't gonna touch us. You wait and see." Then he sat right back in the canoe and opened up a bottle o' beer and took a big quaff like he was old Butterfield or someone.

The wardens come up to about 15 feet of our canoe, and the smell o' skunk paid off jist like Ben was figurin' all the time, and me not knowin' what he was comin' at. They turned off their big lights and sailed right on by jist like they had never even saw us. I and Ben laughed 'til I thought we'd die.

Yes sir, 'twas a lot o' fun.

Herb M. Curtis is the author of six books including three humorous novels. He lives in Fredericton, New Brunswick.

A BOAT NEEDS TO BE BROKEN IN
By Geoff Coleman

If anyone doubts that the north shore of Lake Superior, specifically the Nipigon Bay area, is one of the most compelling places in Canada to fish, consider the actions of Joe Palahnuk as we prepared for an early-summer trip on the big lake.

As Joe and I readied ourselves for the trip, we realized we were going to need some more sinkers. So along with another friend–who wasn't going on the trip but did have a sinker mould–we took to Joe's garage to melt down our supply of lead gleaned from old car batteries, pipes and the dirt backstop of the local target-practice range.

After a couple of hours of heating, pouring, cooling and generally exposing ourselves to lethal fumes, we were well stocked for the upcoming trip. Between the three of us, we had a well-oiled assembly line going, and making the sinkers was anything but work. Joe was enjoying himself so much that he didn't want to quit when we got to the end of our lead supply. Saying something about replenishing our refreshments, he disappeared into the house and came back with five or six bags of store-bought sinkers–the same size and style as we were pouring. "Why don't we melt down these?" he asked.

He could certainly be forgiven for his exuberance. Our outing with Dave Nuttall would take us from the town of Nipigon, into the bay, through the Nipigon Strait, around St. Ignace Island and back to the mainland through the Moffat Strait. Maybe some day we will actually make the complete trip without any major distractions.

A Nipigon Bay trip with Dave guarantees two things–lots of fish and some kind of boat trouble. Nuttall grew up in the area and spends every possible minute of his high-school teacher's summer at his camp/cottage/beach house on Kama Point. Every time Joe and I have been out with him, we have always caught fish–usually lake trout, sometimes a chrome rainbow and, rarely, a big speckled trout.

And just about every time we have been out with him, we have encountered a problem. The *Salvelinus*, after the Latin genus name of the lake and brook trout, is an awesome big-water boat. The 17-foot I/O is uniquely capable of taking the pounding that Superior frequently dishes out, but she is getting a little long in the tooth. Each of the last three annual trips we have made has been spiced up with a near disaster of some sort. Dave's ingenuity and sense of humour, however, prevented each situation from seeming as bad as it really was.

The first time the boat started to show her age was as we steamed through the Nipigon Channel between the Black Bay Peninsula and St. Ignace Island. Dave was telling us about another guy he previously had aboard the *Salvelinus* who simply could not catch a fish. The other two on board were filling the boat using a Kamlooper spoon, but the World's Worst Fisherman couldn't bring himself to switch from the tried-and-true bait he used. After about 15 lakers were caught and released by the others, he relented and cast out a Kamlooper. Sure enough, he got a fish on the first toss. With that one on ice, WWF announced, "Well, now I know they're biting!" and promptly returned to using the old spoon that had been producing like it had soaked overnight in shark repellant. He never caught another fish. (Note to Dave: I realize it was an Alligator spoon.)

Still chuckling over that one, we were drowned out by an ear-piercing noise. It made the sound of the dentist's drill seem like someone waking you up on a Sunday morning with the news they have prepared a pancake breakfast. The unmistakable grinding of fibreglass was followed by a rapid-fire, metallic hammering as the prop tried to slice up a four-billion year-old slab of granite. We were grounded on one of the many shoals that punctuate the channel.

Trimming the load and pushing off with paddles, we freed ourselves and inspected the damage. With no sign of leakage, the hull seemed intact, but the propeller needed replacing. Anyone care to guess the water temperature of Lake Superior in mid-June? Anyone care to guess who had the job of installing the spare propeller? Anyone care to guess how many fish Joe and I caught casting around the shoal while Dave, sans waders, went to work? That was possibly the only time anyone ever earned the $60-dollar an hour labour rate mechanics charge.

Believe it or not, if you had to get lost in the bush with someone, Dave Nuttall is the person you want with you. He is a top-drawer fisherman and hunter, currently holding 19th place on the Pope and Young list of the largest moose ever downed with a bow and arrow. On a previous trip, he skipped us home through these same treacherous waters, in the dark no less, after taking one 10-second glance at our hydrographic chart by the light of a match. I will never understand how he managed, in broad day-light, to miss seeing the buoys that were put out to mark the shoals.

The second indication that the boat was ageing came the following year. We made it through Nipigon Strait safely and rounded St. Ignace Island without incident. Our lazy troll caught us a number of lake trout, but they put up so little resistance, some earned the description, "bag of sand with fins." Thinking we might get a better fight out of a steelhead, we set course for some river mouths on the open-lake side of the island.

As we neared the first mouth, the engine died. Dave vainly tried to start it while I, remembering all the fish I caught while Dave did his mechanic imi-tation last trip, evaluated the fish-catching potential of the location. This particular spot didn't look too inviting, and an offshore wind was threaten-ing to blow us to some great spots on the Michigan side of the lake, so I grabbed a paddle and started us moving toward shore.

As we slowly progressed, Dave removed the engine cover and isolated the problem. It turned out that a two-inch-long pin in the fuel-delivery mechanism had snapped off. In order to get any gas into the carburettor, we would have to come up with a new pin. Dave tried whittling a piece of tree branch to fit, but once it was thin enough to fit the opening, the wood couldn't withstand the stress put on it.

Just as I'm starting to scout for a campsite and a wood supply to last the night, Dave reaches into the toolbox and pulls out a screwdriver. "We are saved!" he proclaims.

It was an interchangeable-bit screwdriver, the kind where the bits are stored in the handle, the kind real craftsmen smirk at. He takes the cap off and removes a bit, which miraculously was the right length and diameter, to replace the broken pin. Dave started the engine, and with a wrap or two of electric tape, his makeshift repair held firm.

Instead of doing the smart thing and heading for home, we trolled over to the river mouth to test Dave's repair job and our steelhead theory. The en-gine ran, and we caught some rainbows, too. Nothing puts the edge on a fight with a steelie like the suspicion in the back of your mind that the en-gine might not start, and that this thing thrashing around like an Olympic gymnast could well be your meal for tonight, and who knows for how long.

The last trip the three of us were on featured unbelievable lake-trout ac-tion. We could do no wrong as every troll across a point brought a strike. We'd land the fish, wheel around and be into another one right away. On one turn, the boat stopped responding to the steering wheel. Joe and I just stepped aside and gave Dave room to diagnose the problem. This time, a broken steering cable.

I'm not sure if Dave was planning for this eventuality, but he had the situation rectified in about 30 seconds. Reaching into the now-legendary toolbox, as a shaman would reach into a medicine chest, he grabbed a box wrench and a pair of vice grips. Moments later he had placed the broken ends of the cable in the openings of the wrench and secured them with a haywire twist. He had the work done so quickly, I was tempted to check the opposite gunwale to see if there was a matching "pike leader on steroids" on the other side of the boat.

After a couple of comments to the effect that he'd be wiser to forget about carrying a tackle box and just throw a couple of lures in his toolbox, we were on our way back to the hot spot. The wrench interfered with the gear-shift cable, so we had to lean over the transom to manually shift the gears on the lower unit, but at least we were able to navigate.

In spite of all these events, I still look forward to our trips. It has long been said there is more to fishing than catching fish, and these outings offer plenty of other things--laughter, adventure, scenic beauty and friendship among them--that put this yearly get-together at the top of my list. I am anticipating it even more this year since Dave tells me he has bought a new boat. Problem is, it's exactly the same model as the last one.

Geoff Coleman is one of Ontario's top outdoor writers with credits in every major fishing magazine. When not fishing, writing or taking pictures, he is a high-school geography teacher in Fenelon Falls, Ontario.

MINDING YOUR MANNERS IN PARADISE

By David Carpenter

When I was a little boy, I had no trouble imagining paradise in very specific terms. No angels and saints for me. My paradise would look just like Johnson Lake, a small reservoir 15 minutes drive from Banff, Alberta, on the Minnewanka Road. It was stocked with rainbow and brook trout that grew prodigiously fast on big nymphs, snails and freshwater shrimp which spawned spring and fall in the feeder stream. I caught my first trout there, and my brother hauled in a six-pound rainbow at the age of six.

When I was in my late teens, I used to fly-fish there with my friend Peter Hyndman. We came to Banff to work in the summer partly because of the fly-fishing. We were just out of high school and convinced that at the secret heart of the unfolding cosmos was nothing but fun. There were more parties in Banff in one month than we had ever gone to at home in a year, more unattached girls than we had ever seen. And one or two nights a week, we would declare a health night and go casting on the banks of Johnson Lake. In my first summer in Banff, I landed a four-pound brook trout, and Hyndman brought in a five-and-a-half-pound rainbow. We were becoming legends in our own time, at least among the trout. The girls were another thing entirely.

Each summer we returned and took the well-worn trail around Johnson Lake. Always there was wildlife. One night a very large black bear came down to the lake to drink or perhaps to stare at the bizarre fly lines whipping through the late-summer air. The bear came right up to me. I think I detected an air of disapproval. This was 1960 or '61 and bears were still so common and innocuous we hadn't learned to fear them. The bear and I looked at each other from a distance of perhaps 20 feet. It saw that I wasn't going to feed it, and so it lumbered off into the jack pine. Hyndman and Carpenter returned to their casting.

A big rainbow was rising just beyond my fly, so I waded in and tried again. Night was falling, and Hyndman had brought in his line.

"One more cast," I told him.

This is the most-commonly-made promise of a fisherman, and the least likely to be honoured. I threw out a big buck tail right where the trout had been rolling in the sunset. I let my line sink and began a slow retrieve. My buck-tail became an escaping minnow. Jerk-jerk-jerk, . . . and suddenly the tip of my rod plunged down. A tail-walking Olympian had grabbed my fly. He leaped high out of the water, paused for a moment to defy gravity and plunged back in. He took off for the middle of the lake and my reel whined, high and frantic.

"Should I get the net?" Hyndman yelled.

"Yes," I must have said to him. "Get the net."

Hyndman got the net and waded over to me while the rainbow cavorted and leaped and took shorter and shorter runs.

"Don't lose him."

Any non-fisher might think this advice was labouring the obvious. But an angler knows this is a good-luck spell one casts for another.

The rainbow seemed to be tiring. It was pointed down and tailing feebly into the gravel. This passive stance allowed me to ease it closer and closer to the net. Hyndman stretched toward the fish. Dark blue on the back, silver on the sides with a long stripe of pink. It was more than two feet long. It was bigger than Hyndman's five-and-a-half-pound rainbow. It was going to be gutted and filled with wild-mushroom stuffing and baked for a gathering of at least a dozen friends. It was going to ingratiate me with a half-dozen mountain beauties and be bragged about for years to . . .

Snap!!!

A side-to-side motion of its head, the rainbow's way of denying a young man's dream of becoming a legend. Gone! The king of the rainbows tailed its way back into the deep water as uncatchable as the great white whale.

One of the differences between old anglers and young anglers is in what they will tell their friends. We told our friends everything about Johnson Lake. We even took them there. We took our girlfriends there, baiting their hooks with big, juicy worms and nymphs. Our friends told their friends and their friends told their friends. By the mid-'60s, this lake, which I felt Hyndman and I had owned, became host to dozens of anglers a day and one or two wild parties each night in the campground. You could hear the voices of folk singers and the sound of guitars and bongos. Always those plaintive, undergraduate voices puling about the misfortunes of picking cotton in the hot sun or mining for coal. I was one of those folk singers.

I even remember once throwing a half-finished bottle of wine into the lake. Someone had noticed the approach of an RCMP patrol car, and I was under age. I threw the bottle into the lake in panic, and stumbled off into the woods. The wine in question was pink, cheap and bubbly and called crackling rosé. Does anyone else remember crackling rosé?

The problem with paradise is always the people who go there.

Johnson Lake declined rapidly as a fishing spot, and by the mid-1970s it was only good for a few trout of the pan-size variety. By and by, the parks people stopped stocking it.

By the mid-1980s, I had given up on Johnson Lake. It was overfished, and the only catchable trout seemed to be spawners. And then an incredible thing happened. I was driving by one evening for a nostalgic look at the lake of my youth. At most I'd hoped to get a glimpse of an osprey or a rising trout. I parked my car in a newly constructed parking lot with signs and fancy latrines and picnic benches. I took our old path to the rise overlooking the lake. I looked at the lake.

More accurately, I looked *for* the lake. In the evening light it appeared to be gone. Perhaps I blinked or shook my head. It *was* gone. The dam at the near end of the lake had burst, leaving behind an ugly grey scar. A prank I was told later. I raced down to what had been the shore of the lake. I leaped into the muddy cavity. I walked all the way down to the middle of the lake to what would have been one of the biggest holes. All I could find was a trickle from the feeder stream.

How many magnificent memories had that lake held? Standing in the muddy bottom, I had a last look and slowly trudged back. Perhaps a hundred feet from shore my foot dislodged something that made me look down. A wine bottle. It was unbroken and it had no label. But I could tell at a glance from the shape and colour that it had once been a bottle of crackling rosé. I suppose it could have been the bottle of some other folk singer, equally drunk and irresponsible, but I think it was mine. I took the bottle, communed with it for a while and threw it into the garbage container next to my car. But the bottle wouldn't go away. It contained messages from those carefree years: 1960, 1961, 1962, 1963, 1964, 1965 . . . Michael row your boat ashore, Hallelujah . . .

This story began with the discovery of my wine bottle. The lake of all memories seemed to disgorge a sad and bounteous flow of them. I had heard often enough that the mind is like a lake that harbours memories in the great unconscious. But now it seemed to me that the lake was like a huge mind. The more I looked at its vast, muddy, grey container, the more it poured out the ghosts of its former life, and mine. I was saddened by the usual things: the loss of youth, the loss of that feeling that the sky was the limit, the inevitable comparisons between the bounteous past and the fishless present. But I think what bothered me most of all was that I had betrayed my lake. I'd made it known to mobs of people unworthy of its great gifts. I'd conspired against my lake by leaving my trash in it and using it merely for my pleasure. I had not taken the time or made the effort to become my lake's custodian.

Stories like this are legion, and they almost always end with a sad nostalgic sigh. But this one doesn't. A few weeks ago, I was in Banff on business. The town had transformed from a place where families came to stay and see the wonders of nature, to a place where wealthy foreigners came to shop. Walking down Banff Avenue was agony. I decided to get out of town and go for a drive. It was more habit than intention that took me out to Johnson Lake, and there I made another amazing discovery–it was once again brim-full of water and trout! If there's a god that presides over this earthly paradise, he works for the fisheries department and stocks fish for a living. He is the Johnny Appleseed of the freshwater kingdom. God bless him wherever he goes.

If you should happen to come upon my new, old lake, you'll have no problem recognizing me. I'm the balding guy in the belly boat who floats like a frog and hums old folk songs. I'll watch how you dispose of your garbage, whether you stick to your limit, whether you bring a ghetto blaster to drown out the sounds of the wilderness, whether you tear up the trail with your ATV. If you fail any of my tests, I will be unforgiving. If you're foolish enough to throw a bottle into the lake, beware. You may not see me *do* anything, but if a huge bear should amble down to your campsite and send you up a tree, don't say I didn't warn you.

David Carpenter is a Saskatoon, Saskatchewan, writer. His works of fiction include *God's Bedfellows* and *Jokes for the Apocalypse.* His latest book is *Fishing in the West.*

RIMSHOT
By Ray Dillon

I can still recall my childhood quite vividly, waking to the sound of a strutting rooster crowing on our small farm, the taste of freshly baked rhubarb dumpling smothered in cream, the feel of cool, dark earth pushed up between my toes from a new-ploughed field. It was a Walt Disney kind of childhood, and on many occasions, I half expected Old Yeller to come barking and tail-wagging out of our woods.

The truth of the matter was that we were only small-time farmers, dirt poor and hard working. When my daddy didn't have chores for me to do, he'd make up some. "Go get the wood in for night, boy!" he'd yell from the stable.

"Already did, Dad," I'd reply.

"Well, then, go start cuttin' some for next winter," he'd come back.

The joys of being brought up on a farm were few, and the work was hard, but I grew steadily and strongly, none the worse for the wear and tear.

A small creek cut across our property, dissecting one field and snaking through the woods and the cedar swamp beyond, and it was there that I learned to fish. Many an enjoyable afternoon was spent with jeans rolled up to my knees and my bare feet dangling in the creek. One of my favourite fishing holes was quite deep, maybe five feet or so, along one bank. It had washed out under the bank, and lots of small trout lurked in the shadows of two huge cedars that overhung the pool. I often dreamed of raising my very own big trout in that pool, but I was ten years old before it became a reality.

One morning the opportunity came to fish the big river several miles from our farm. A friend and his dad were going down there trout fishing and invited me along. I grabbed my alder pole and bait can but also brought along an old galvanized pail we watered cows with. Before the morning was up, I had a twelve-incher in the pail, ready to stock my own creek.

The fishing trip was exciting except for Billy's father always telling us to be careful and not to fall into the river, and I took extreme pleasure in seeing him do a double gainer into the ledge pool, right in front of us. We both laughed hysterically after we saw he was all right.

The trip homeward seemed to take ages, but just before dark on that late-May evening, I revived this big brookie and tossed him into the pool by the cedars. It was the beginning of a long and peculiar friendship. Now to have a fish as a pet, especially when the pet owner loves fishing, was strange, but this fish was no ordinary fish. I was learning basketball fundamentals in school, so I called this trout Rimshot.

Rimshot had strange-looking eyes, unlike any trout I had ever seen. His orbs were kind of whitish, and when he looked at you, he kind of reminded you of a dead fish rather than a live one. To have two white fish eyes staring at you was sometimes unnerving, but I never let him know. When I'd feed him, I'd often turn away so he wouldn't see the look of fear and disgust on my face. What seemed to be worse was that Rimshot had a depth-perception problem. He'd swim around the pool jumping for flies and missing them. He also had the nasty habit of running into things both in the water and when he'd jump.

On several occasions, I found Rimshot lying on his side, unconscious in the pool or on the shore. Once I gave him mouth-to-mouth to resuscitate him, and man it was awful! He tasted real fishy, and with those whitish eyes just staring, I wasn't sure if I was making progress or not until he moved his tail fin slightly. The damned fish would chase frogs and water spiders, and of course, they knew there was something wrong with him. They'd lead him a merry chase around the pool and into the rocks, and first thing you know, bang old Rimshot would swim headlong into one of those rocks.

My trout grew as summer progressed, and I taught him to jump up after fish pellets. He seemed to have a keen sense of hearing, and he'd actually respond when I called his name. "Here, Rimshot. Come get your supper." It was so nice to see him come darting out from the shadows and then to watch him jump. Oh yes, he'd occasionally hit one of the cedars, and I'd have to revive him, but most times, he'd grab those pellets right out of my hand. His head and face were scarred awfully from all the times he ran into rocks and trees, but for two years he survived and grew despite his handicap. By his second year, he was 17 inches long and weighed in at about three pounds.

Rimshot had eaten most of the smaller fish and ruled the pool. I had found an old basketball net rim and nailed it to one of the cedars. I made a small platform on the edge and encouraged my fish to jump through the hoop and grab fish pellets as he went. Poor old Rimshot beat his head and face severely on the rim of that hoop, to the point I worried someone would discover what was taking place there and report me to the SPCF–the Society for the Prevention of Cruelty to Fish. It was innocent enough, but Rimshot's eyesight was getting worse and his head-butting into rocks and trees, more frequent.

I often fished that creek in other areas, when my chores and Dad would allow, and despite the changing of the seasons, I'd always catch my limit of fat brookies. Still none were even half the size of the king of the Cedar Pool, and every chance I got, I'd place food on that old basketball hoop for my buddy.

Over the space of three summers, Rimshot embarrassed me only twice that I can recall. Once we had pet day at school, an opportunity to bring in our favourite pet to tell about him and show him off. I carried Rimshot in a five-gallon bucket. My teacher, old Mrs. Hornby, looked down her nose at the trout in my pail as though she thought I was pulling a bad joke. As she peered over the top of her glasses, the light caught them just right, and they glittered like light on a lure. Rimshot leaped for what he thought was food and knocked Mrs. Hornby on her posterior. Although it was amply padded, the laughter of the class and the fact that she had fish slime on her face incited Mrs. Hornby to seek revenge. "I'll have that damned fish for supper," she roared, and had I not scurried home with my pet, she undoubtedly would have done so.

The second occasion was one morning when a friend of Dad's came to have his cow bred. He brought his pretty, young daughter, and both of them insisted that we go and do something, far away from the barn. The dandelions were splashed through acres of blowing grass, and daisies and brown-eyed susans turned the pasture into cow-paddy heaven. When Prissy asked what was going on at the barn, I took on my deepest pre-puberty voice and explained the facts of life to this little brunette.

"You see, Prissy, your dad's got a cow, and my dad's got a bull. When your cow wants to have a little cow, my dad leads her to his bull. They sniff noses and bawl a lot. Our bull jumps on your cow, trying to get her to lie down. She won't, though, not 'til they're married. Then she goes home with your dad and has a baby." The explanation was as close as I could come to the reason why cows have babies, and it seemed to satisfy her. Eventually we arrived at the stream. Rimshot was ready to perform for food, and I would soon be totally embarrassed.

Prissy thought it was great that I had a pet trout, and that made me feel really proud. I couldn't help noticing that Prissy was beginning to bud out and that two white roses decorated her blouse in the right places to emphasize her burgeoning womanhood. I gave her a handful of fish pellets and encouraged her to lean over and place them on the basketball hoop. As she did so, Rimshot noticed the flowers or the food or both. He leaped from the dark water and latched onto her blouse and the tiny nipple under the rose. What was worse, he hung on, flapping about as she screamed. "Let go of her you crazy fish!" I yelled and moved to her side.

The episode still burns fresh in my memory, and the embarrassment of having to brush her bosom several times to free her from that perverted fish's grasp overwhelms me. She ran from the pool with a slimy mouthprint on her new blouse, and her father wasn't too impressed with my story of what had happened. "Should kill that pervert fish," he grumbled to my dad.

Dad just stood there and shook his head. "I won't charge you for getting her bred," he said. "A-h-h-h-h, I mean the cow."

I knew those carefree summers had been too good to be true and were about to come to an end. A new preacher had come to our community and was intent on saving my soul. In fact, he was determined to chase the Devil clean out of the county, or so he said. Mama was a good, God-fearing woman and Dad was, well, he wasn't a heathen.

The Reverend had heard about my tryst with Prissy, and somehow the story had been changed. Although people don't intentionally lie, they occasionally distort the truth to sensationalize it. If you don't believe me, tell someone a joke. By the time you hear it again, you won't recognize it. At any rate, the Rev had heard that I took Prissy to the back 40 and had my way with her while our bull was doing her cow. "I shall save the boy from a life of iniquity and sin," he assured my mother, who was now starting to believe the rumours.

It was a beautiful Saturday morning when the preacher came by. He went in and prayed with, or preyed on, my dad and mom, and then took Dad up on his offer to fish our creek. "You know, Jesus was a fisherman, as were Peter and John," he grinned, baiting his hook. I was guiding him along our creek. "You can fish anywhere but that big pool there with the basketball hoop and the cedars," I told him.

"You run along boy, and I'll teach you later," the Rev grinned. "I'm gonna catch supper for your family."

Dad yelled for me to go weed the garden, so I ran back through the fields to the barn and the garden plot at the side, relieved to be out of the hellfire stare of that man with the booming voice.

I had finished the eighth row of vegetables when Mama yelled that supper was on. It looked like a storm was brewing, and a slight breeze came from the north-east. That usually meant rain and always worried me. A swollen creek could sweep Rimshot away. What was worse, if Rimshot got scared by the thunder and lightning, he might leap out of the water and hit a tree and maybe lie there like a big, fishy lightning rod, getting barbecued by a stray lightning bolt.

As I went to the house to wash up for supper, I prayed, "Please Sir, don't let nothin' hurt my fish. He doesn't mean to be bad. It's just that he's only got a little fish brain, and he don't know what's right or what's wrong. Keep him nice 'n warm tonight, and don't let him wash away in no flood. Put him 'n an ark, Lord," and with that I entered the dining room.

The Rev sat beside my dad at the head of the table wearing a smug grin. Mama was carrying in great bowls of potatoes and vegetables, a platter of hot biscuits and a brimming gravy boat. The final dish came to the table, strangely unrecognizable. It was a large wooden platter shaped like an arc, and it had large fish steaks steaming under the cover. "Gee Mom, where'd you get the neat bowl?" I asked.

"It was a gift from Reverend Smee," she smiled, "and he caught the fish for supper, too." We filled our plates and Mom opened the arc for trout.

Suddenly those fish steaks were piecing together in my mind. I reached out and placed the steaks end to end. There was something awful familiar on that platter. "Oh my God, Rimshot! God, I asked you to put him in an ark and keep him warm, but you cooked him up!" I rushed from the table out to the porch.

The Rev and Mom and Dad came rushing out after me. "You all right, boy?" Dad asked. "Yeah, son, what's goin' on?" Mom asked.

"It's the work of the Devil!" the Rev bellowed. It's funny how you grow to hate someone who can't talk without hollering and uttering threats, especially when they killed your pet trout. I ran to the barn in the pouring rain, with the preacher following me. "Don't fret over that fish, boy, he was the best one I've ever caught. You can get yourself another one."

I collected my thoughts, my memories of Rimshot. Those whitish, ghouly eyes, his problem with depth and distance perception, all the times I had found him knocked out in the water and on the creek banks. I cried some and I laughed some. Man, I had really hated to administer mouth-to-mouth that time . . . and him latching onto Prissy's tit, er, nipple, er, mammary gland.

127

I looked up at the holier-than-thou preacher. "Ya got a pet, preach'?" I sneered.

"Oh, yeah, I got myself a nice white cat," he said.

I said quietly, "Someday bring her over, and I'll teach her to swim."

Ray Dillon owns and operates Malarkey Cabin Guiding Service at Zealand, New Brunswick, and is a licensed fishing and hunting guide.

BEYOND THE CALL OF DUTY
By Ron Miller

Lt. Col. William Lockwood Muncie, U.S. Army (Ret.), sat tensed and alert in the stern of his cedar-strip canoe watching his braided 20-pound-test line as it disappeared into the boulder-strewn depths of Rowan Lake. Presently a floating loop of the heavy, black line twitched and straightened, scattering glistening droplets of spray as the Colonel set the hook with a mighty sweep of the heavy rod. The five pound lake trout was no match for the Colonel's heavy tackle and soon lay flopping in the bottom of the canoe.

The Colonel had fished our trout waters regularly for many seasons, and over the years, we had come to know that if there was anything he loved more than catching, cooking and eating lake trout, it was blowing his bugle. Early in his military career, the Colonel had been a bugler, and now, some 50 years later, his old battered and bent cavalry bugle was as much a part of his kit as his ancient True Temper steel casting rod and the venerable Pflueger Supreme reel. Attired in his stiff-brimmed campaign hat, checked shirt, corduroy breeches and laced, high-top boots, he resembled a character brought to life from the pages of a 1939 sporting-goods catalogue.

These biannual quests for trout would usually see the Colonel in the company of several of his cronies. They would meet at the float-plane base in Nestor Falls, Ont., for the 30 minute flight to the lodge, but not so the good Colonel. You see, he just didn't feel comfortable in those new-fangled contraptions and preferred to take an extra day and paddle his old varnished cedar-strip down through the rugged chain of lakes, eventually arriving at our landing on the Rowan Lake portage.

His arrival was always heralded by the staccato notes of the old bugle as he set the jack pines ringing with the cavalry "Charge!" A grand entrance indeed!

Plunging his paddle into the calm surface of the lake, the Colonel sent the canoe skimming toward the spruce and balsam-studded island a hundred yards distant. The island with its flat, granite shelf and the circle of fire-blackened stones had been the scene of many grand and glorious shore lunches, and today was no exception. Shore lunch for the Colonel and his gang was a tradition not to be taken lightly, and was a ritual eagerly awaited by all hands.

Colonel Bill ceremoniously built a driftwood cook fire in the circle of blackened stones, and from the depths of his First World War-vintage duffel bag produced one of his most-prized possessions–a chipped and dinged, smoke-blackened stewpot.

With military precision, the Colonel slowly added the ingredients that made up his secret trout chowder. When all was ready, he moved the brimming stewpot to the outer edge of the coals so the mix wouldn't scorch.

The Colonel stood for a moment on the edge of the rocky shelf absorbing the magnificent tranquility of his surroundings. Majestic pines thrust cathedral-like spires into an azure sky. The chalky, bone-white trunks of birch reflected off the water with the clarity of fine crystal.

Putting the mouthpiece of the old bugle to his lips, he sent the familiar "Mess Call" resounding out in clarion tones. Before the last notes had died away, the drone of outboard motors could be heard churning their way toward the Colonel and the steaming cauldron of chowder. Colonel Bill and his army dined in regal fashion indeed!

It is not to say that the Colonel held all modern technology in contempt. In some respects, he was as modern as tomorrow. However, when it came to catching lake trout, he spurned the tackle and techniques favoured by his associates: the graphite and boron rods, spinning reels and monofilament line, jigs and silver-plated flutter spoons. Their sophisticated depth sounders, down riggers and side planners he viewed with utter disdain. The Colonel maintained that to catch one fish with his simplistic approach was worth more to him than taking a dozen by any other method. He reasoned that one day he would likely land the trophy that had so far eluded him, the one trout that would make all the others pale by comparison, the one bragging-size trout that would rest on its plaque over his mantel.

As all his well-fed friends roared back up-lake, Colonel Bill tossed his pack into the old canoe. Quietly he paddled back to his favourite spring trout flats–a twelve-foot-deep stretch of water, strewn with massive boulders, bordering a deep water drop-off.

The day seemed to pass all too soon, and the sun rested like a polished brass disc on the western horizon. Purple shadows crept slowly from the darkening shore as the Colonel fished beneath a twilight sky. "One more drift," he thought to himself. One more drift and then a pleasant paddle back to the lodge and the tall tales, old friends and a good supper.

Stiff and unresponsive as it was, the Colonel felt comfortable with his old, steel rod. Since its purchase sometime back in the '40s, he had come to know the feel of a gentle bait pick-up, as well as the unrelenting tug of a snag among the boulders. And now as the heavy rod bent slightly and the old level-wind reel slowly clicked, the Colonel was prepared to end the day with an obvious, yet disappointing, break off.

But wait! Could it be? Did that "snag" move ever so slightly? Yes! Again the line moved. This time with a sureness, an authority, the Colonel had never before experienced. Fighting an almost overwhelming urge to strike, the Colonel stripped line from the reel, a little more, more yet–wait, wait just a bit longer. He watched with steely concentration as the heavy, black line slipped slowly into the depths. A pause, a slight hesitation and then– STRIKE! The old True Temper arched and set the line quivering tight! The sturdy Pflueger screamed in protest as it gave up yard after yard of hissing line. The old soldier, with jaw set and knuckles gone white, was engaged in the most classic of all one-on-one encounters–the man and the fish!

Slowly but surely, this yet unseen leviathan was towing the Colonel and the canoe into deeper waters. Fifty feet, 60, 70, the fish now lay sounding on the bottom. Pump and reel, pump and reel. The old man was gaining ever so little, but gaining he was! And now in the fading light, eight or maybe 10 feet under the canoe, Colonel Bill could see, almost with disbelief, his great, silvery, deep-bellied opponent. The fish, it seemed, had seen the Colonel as well, and with a strength born of desperation plunged again toward the bottom.

The fish was tiring but possibly not as much as the Colonel. A moment's lack of concentration, a split second of inspired overconfidence, and the Colonel's burning thumb clamped tightly–too tightly–on the gyrating spool. Maybe it was metal fatigue, maybe it was the tortuous stress the Colonel and the fish had put on the old rod. With a sickening snap, it broke cleanly just before the reel seat.

The Colonel reached frantically for the broken section as it slid down the line. Throwing the now useless reel and rod handle aside, he held tightly to the heavy nylon line. Blood dripped from his fingers as the line cut into his hand.

Colonel Bill was a competent canoeist, but the epic battle caused him to lurch heavily. The gunwale dipped, and the frigid waters of Rowan Lake surged into the canoe. One second? Two? How long does it take to live a nightmare? The cedar-strip rolled, and the Colonel was flung headlong into the icy waters. Bill Muncie clung desperately to the overturned canoe with one hand and struggled to maintain his grip on the line with the other. Fortunately the gentle breeze drifted him slowly toward the shallow and rocky shore of the island.

In what seemed like hours, but actually was only moments, the Colonel felt the slippery shoreline boulders under his feet. Staggering in the shallows, he fell to his knees and slowly began to retrieve the line–foot by foot, yard by yard. He was exhausted. But then so was his opponent.

The light was nearly gone as the two powerboats idled along the shoreline. The Colonel's buddies shouted and called his name. They knew he was usually off the water by this time, and his absence was cause for concern. They spotted the canoe first, half submerged and gently tossing on the rocks near shore.

"There he is! Hey, Bill you okay?"

The boats drew near, and the men jumped out into the knee-deep shallows. The Colonel sat motionless, the giant trout clutched to his chest. "Lord o' mercy, Bill! You got him! The one you been after all these years! Man, he's gonna look good over your fireplace!"

Colonel Bill loosened his grasp on the great fish, slipping the hook from its jaw, and slowly lowered the monster tenderly into the water. The men watched as the gills slowly opened and closed then pumped in a steady and rhythmic cadence. Then with a thrust of its powerful tail, the big fish glided majestically into the deepening waters and was gone.

A single droplet of moisture ran unnoticed down the old man's cheek, disappearing in the stubble on his chin. Maybe it was just a drop of lake water, maybe not.

It was the first day of September when the letter came. The return address on the envelope was familiar, but the handwriting was foreign to me. The words were stiff and formal, and the message painfully clear. The Colonel wouldn't be coming to fish this fall, not in this life, anyway. Colonel Bill, at 81 years old had answered that final call to muster.

Somewhere in the deep and secret depths of Rowan Lake, there remains a smoke-stained enamelware stewpot, a corroding brass bugle and a 37-pound lake trout. Should some day a lucky individual recover any one of the three, he will have taken a cherished trophy indeed.

Ron Miller is an award-winning outdoor writer, columnist and broadcaster, Past President and Life Member of the Outdoor Writers of Canada. He lives in Winnipeg, Manitoba.

DOWN-UNDER ANGLERS UP HERE
By Lyn Hancock

"Going to Great Bear Lake?" smiled the agent at the Canadian North Airlines counter in Yellowknife as she checked our fishing rods.

Mum, dressed determinedly in a skirt and high heels, despite her wilderness destination and my remonstrations, looked at the gaggle of 67 happy-go-lucky fishermen behind us and asked apprehensively, "Any other women on your list?"

The agent laughed and shook her head. "No, and you're the only Australians. Don't worry. You're in for a good time."

I could think of no better place to take my parents for a once-in-a-lifetime fishing trip than Chummy Plummer's prestigious lodge on Great Bear Lake. At the time of their visit, Dad had shingles and Mum was suffering from what later was diagnosed as cancer, but these two doughty adventurers would let nothing interfere with their trip to the fishing Mecca of the Northwest Territories.

Deep, cold, crystal-clear Great Bear Lake, the fourth-largest lake in North America, and the Arctic oasis of Tree River, 232 miles to the north-east, are known around the world for consistent catches of big, wild fish. Lots of them. Trophy fish such as a 74-pound lake trout, a 32-pound 9-ounce Arctic char and a five-pound 15-ounce grayling. And northern pike. And whitefish.

The Plummers who own one lodge on Great Bear Lake and manage all five, are legends in fishing circles. They have 50 years' experience catering to a world clientele, and they run a fleet of boats and planes to get their guests and guides to the best fishing spots. Their private 737-jet service direct to their lodge from Winnipeg and Yellowknife is unique in the industry, and their accommodations, according to the brochures, were luxurious–which is why my mother insisted on her skirt and high heels. (When she set down on the tundra above the Arctic Circle she did change to long johns and "those awful rubber boots.")

Back home, Mum and Dad are legends themselves. In the '50s when his business associates were dying from stress-related heart attacks, Dad put a sign on the store, Gone Fishing. At 45, he and Mum retired. He studied their bank account and figured he could get in "five bloody good years fishing." Five years stretched to 10 and then to 35. Needless to say, my parents ate–and still eat–a lot of fish.

Now in their 80s, Mum and Dad spend summers in the south of Western Australia living aboard a 21-foot boat anchored off Rottnest Island and winters in the north, living in a 16-foot caravan at Coral Bay with a dinghy at the door. They go daily into the Indian Ocean where others do not dare.

Aussies are still talking of the day my parents caught the giant cod. Dad and Mum were fishing from their dinghy, as usual, with handlines in 150 feet of rough ocean, 10 miles beyond the reef in a place named The Mixing Bowl for its tempestuous waters. Suddenly, a monster took Dad's line.

Fortunately, Dad had been hoping for a 50-pound red emperor so he had 500 yards of 100-pound-test line and a number-70 hook on his simple wooden reel. He needed the lot.

It took Dad an hour to bring in that fish–pulling as fast as he could in the bobbing dinghy, searing through two sets of gloves, straining against the gunwale, trying to keep his feet steady and the line from tangling around his body as the fish ran and dodged and twisted in its efforts to get away. "At one point, I was sure that fish was taking us to Africa. I kept praying the line wouldn't snag or snap on a spike of coral," he said later.

Finally, Dad got it alongside. "It was a slimy cod, almost grouper size." To get it back to the beach he put half hitches through its cheeks, secured it by a cleat to the transom then increased his speed to 10 knots until the fish planed behind.

"I had trouble keeping its mouth out of water so it didn't go under and drag down the dinghy–and of course, fending off the sharks," Dad told me.

His reputation as "the old man of the sea" escalated considerably when his cod was pulled out of the ocean by truck and winched onto the scales. "It had to be a hell of a lot more than 300 pounds–the fillets were 50 pounds–but that's as far as the scale went. It was too big really, too tough. Not nice eating at all," he recalled.

My parents' fishing methods are simple and economic. Drifting over the reef, jigging with hooks, line and sinker, hoping for whiting, skipjack and snapper but taking anything that comes along–rock cod, herring or parrot fish. Trolling at two miles an hour with the line enclosed by such home-made lures as red and white drinking straws. (Who needs a half wave or red devil spoon?) Chumming by wrapping berley around a piece of meat bait or scattering it on the water to attract schooling fish. (Berley is a sticky concoction of "chook" or chicken food–bran and pollard, egg, flour and water. Each person has his or her own recipe.)

They are expert with hooks, lines and sinkers but they have no experience with rods and reels. Not wanting to embarrass them in front of the seasoned anglers at Great Bear Lake, I outfitted them with the best of my fishing buddies' recommendations.

We arrived at Plummers' with Shimano's state-of-the-art Aero reels with their one-handed quick-fire cast that I hoped would defy Mum's arthritic fingers, Berkley's 4-6-8and 12-pound-test line (pragmatic Dad thought 50-pound line would be better), snap swivels and barbless hooks. We also had what was to Dad a bewildering variety of lures–Len Thompson's ubiquitous five of diamonds and red devil, several intriguing Mepps and Williams kits, one for each species, and a vast assortment of Rapalas (which to Dad at least looked like fish.) Added to those were more we bought at the lodge: large spoons such as red eyes, daredevils and half waves, and rubbery eel-like jigs such as puddle jumpers and white reapers. Fishing didn't seem simple any more.

It also seemed serious business. Our gear was quickly whisked by truck to our cabins. We were whisked another way by boat to a big welcome buffet in the dining room. Mum's biggest surprise was finding a waitress from her home town willing to share her treasured jar of Vegemite, a gooey, black yeast condiment only an Aussie could love.

We were in the boats within an hour of landing on the airstrip.

"You don't need those Rapalas," said my guide, Gerard, a 21-year-old fishing fanatic who told me that back home in Ottawa he had 18 Shimano rods and reels (I scored with him on that point.) "Those floaters are fine if the trout are feeding at the surface and they're great for bass and wall-eye down east but up here, at this time of the year, we'll be fishing for the big ones in cold, deep water by drop-offs, say 18 feet to 100 feet."

Gerard sensed our hesitation at abandoning the bulk of our fishing supplies and allowed us to bring aboard all the Rapala deep runners. Ironically, my first fish that afternoon–a nine-pound red fin lake trout–was lured by a silver shad rap Rapala.

Anyway, in the week at Great Bear we got to use them all–the contents of our tackle boxes, those of the guides, some of the other guests and a goodly selection from the lodge's Trading Post. "Just yank it out and slap on another lure, it's easier than a hand line and more of a challenge," said Gerard nonchalantly every time we lost one. Mike, an Ojibway from Sioux

Narrows who'd been coming to Plummer's for decades, didn't talk much. He just did it. So did George, our Inuit guide from Coppermine. Obviously our guides were not children of the depression.

Down under, Mum and Dad would probably spend hours with a water-glass bending over the side, staring into the clear, warm waters of the reef and directing the dinghy back and forth till the hook wiggled clear. That would be wasted fishing time up here.

I think the guides ran an informal competition to see whose customers got the most and the biggest fish. If so, we probably disappointed them by not having our lines in the water as many times as everybody else. Some of those who did reported a strike every two minutes. One angler in Neiland Bay got 63 lake trout, 28 of them over 20 pounds. He and his 10 companions tallied 595 trout for the week, with 82 over 20 pounds.

Down under where they fish all year, Mum and Dad are certainly up before dawn to check and bait their crayfish (alias saltwater lobster) pots but they restrict fishing to before lunch and again after supper. But at Plummer's, meals were too good to miss ("You mean a whole chicken to yourself?" Mum marvelled at a Cornish game hen on her plate.) And the long evenings were good for hot tubbing, watching Arctic ground squirrels skitter between burrows, eagles perch on picturesque trees or caribou stroll the airstrip.

We did practise using our fishing gear but in the privacy of our cabin with the line hooked to a chair. "I don't want Mike to think me a mug," moaned Mum who bewailed her arthritic fingers.

Despite our low ranking as dedicated anglers, our guides and pilots were unfailingly polite and obliging, even though I had valiant Gerard manning the motor, my cameras and my fishing rod, sometimes all at the same time; Mum had Mike casting her lure and Dad had him extricating knots.

Other anglers encouraged us to have fun by playing our fish with a light rod and line. Trouble was that my parents were more used to the big, the bold and the primitive, not the fine, the finicky and the technological. They found that spin casting was a lot of work. Despite her inexperience with sophisticated Shimanos, Mum caught more fish than Dad and I put together.

They weren't trophies like the woman who got a 46-pound lake trout near the main lodge after ice-out or the man who got a 66-1/2-pound world record a week later. Hers weren't much more than 10-pounders but they were all good fighters, and she was excited by every one. Dad and I even got some beautiful three and four-pound grayling. And in contrast to other anglers, especially Canadians, their greatest thrill came from catching–and eating–the lowly, long-underestimated pike. Unbelievably, they preferred it to char.

My parents' only complaint was that their catch was whisked away before they had really looked at it. Under the lodge's strict catch-and-release policy, termed "hug-and-release" at Plummer's, the guides had them nursed lovingly back to the water almost before they were out of it. Shore lunch was their only opportunity to study the fish and then, to my frugal parents, there seemed an overabundance, an irony they could not figure out.

Another irony was my parents' habit of killing food fish immediately, contrasted sharply with the guides' habit of letting shore lunch fish expire slowly at the bottom of the boat. And, shades of animal rights activists, Mum wondered how anglers considered it sport to "play" and tire out a fish intentionally on light tackle.

Do I *have* to throw it back?" Mum asked plaintively when up came her first lake trout within moments of putting her lure in the water. Mike had to prise it from her hands. "That fish is certainly lucky," she said watching it revive and slip away. "It killed me to throw mine back," Dad confided to me later.

They were pretty fish. Gerard pointed to the local variants. "Bluebacks" were standard and meant what they said. "Red fins" had distinct red fin tips and a splotched brown, grey and white lateral line. "Feather fins" had huge fins resembling feathers when pulled apart. Not only are the fins quite red on these Great Bear Lake trout but the flesh is bright red too. Like salmon–which of course they are.

We didn't have to worry about throwing fish back on our overnight trip by DC-3 to fish for char at Tree River. Unfortunately we didn't catch any.

It should have been easy. Surprisingly hot Aussie-type weather almost good enough for shorts. No long bumpy boat rides to spread the fishing pressure as at Great Bear Lake. We had only to stand on the riverbank close to our tent door and cast into the rapids. Dozens of magnificently-coloured, hook-jawed Arctic char churned the waters into froth as they literally leaped along the rushing river to spawn. Others rested in the bottom of quiet pools, some close enough to touch. One week later, there'd be even more.

"Tree River's the place to clean out your tackle box," said Chummy Plummer. "If you're not losing lures, you're not where the fish are," said the game warden who to Dad's absolute amazement had a shack on "this river way up in never-never land" with binoculars trained on the main fishing spots.

The hot spot was Mercer Point named after a guest who'd been coming to Plummer's for 30 years. Thirteen anglers and three Inuit guides crowded onto the little beach. The current was strong, the water shallow and the bottom rocky. If you didn't hook a rock you hooked line from dozens of anglers who had stood there before. Mum, Dad and I kept George constantly busy yanking out lures and unravelling line (at last we could use our 12 and 15-pound line) but unfortunately not netting char.

For the first few hours, the wind and tide churned up the silt to murk and the visually oriented char couldn't strike, but then the wind subsided, the waters cleared and the run was on.

I wish Mum and Dad had tied into one of those leaping char. They told me once that pulling up fish in Canada was like pulling up logs. They couldn't say that about the fish in Great Bear Lake or Tree River.

We certainly cleaned out our tackle box–rat'l 'n trap Rapalas, Mepps spinners, pixie and daredevil spoons, all of Mr. Ensley's reapers (char tend to bite off their plastic tails) and several heavy white polar-bear-fur jigs which were hooking 20-pounders for two keen anglers from Pennsylvania.

My parents gave up the struggle. I fished on. No char. It was beginning to be embarrassing. Nearly everybody had landed fish but us. Some of the Americans offered us theirs. Fortunately we knew the regulations and declined. Very fortunately. The week before, a high-ranking government official, who should have known better, was charged–and later convicted– of being in possession of illegal fish. He had accepted a legal fish from his buddy, and it was recorded by the dedicated fisheries officer on the hill behind.

It was time to go. The others left to pack up their gear, have lunch and head for the airstrip. I stayed and lost more lures to those maddening red flashes in front of me. Al, the pilot, was thundering down the runway before I gave up.

It didn't matter, really. "Tree River's not just fishing, it's the total experience," Chummy had said. We were there only 24 hours, but it was jam-packed with memories.

Some great fishing buddies (fishing's a great leveller.) A hike across the tundra to look at old graves. A walk with George to photograph several waterfalls upriver. A drop-in visit to an Inuit camp downriver. A sightseeing flight along the Arctic coast and Bloody Fall on the Coppermine River. A tour of Coppermine itself.

And some unexpected highlights. Dad, an old biker, commandeered an all-terrain vehicle from an Inuk on the Coppermine airstrip and got to go for a ride, a long-cherished dream. Mum got to do girl talk with some Inuit mothers outside the Co-op and was assured that no, the babies in their parka hoods did not get smothered.

We all gained a lot.

I learned how fragile a treasure is each of our myriad northern lakes and rivers, how those who have lost such pristine waters elsewhere are the most dedicated champions of their conservation. And I learned to look at fish with the same care and concern that I have automatically for other creatures.

My parents went back to Australia with changed attitudes, a deeper appreciation for what they still have Down under, and a deeper understanding for the stringent regulations and higher prices up here.

Dad admitted that fishing at home was not as good as it used to be. More people, more boats, more roads to the fishing spots. Fewer fish, smaller fish, longer time to fill your freezer with fillets.

"And you know, looking back, it was exciting bringing in that cod, but we should have let it go. It was probably a hundred years old. It could have had another 50-60 years."

Lyn Hancock is an award-winning freelance writer and photographer and author of a dozen books including *There's A Seal In My Sleeping Bag, There's A Raccoon In My Parka, Love Affair With A Cougar, An Ape Came Out Of My Hatbox, The Mighty Mackenzie, Tell Me, Grandmother, Northwest Territories, Alaska Highway and Looking For The Wild.* She lives in Fort Simpson, North West Territories and Mill Bay, British Columbia.

AT LIAR'S ROCK
By Wayne Curtis

Liar's Rock is gone now, pushed away through the years by the ice jams, like so many lesser stones. Gone, too, are the many fishermen, outfitters and guides that gave the great rock its name. It was flat on top, like a bed, with a curved place to lie upon. In 1960 it was located at the centre of the long gravel beach at the Gray Rapids salmon pool on the Miramichi. Paul O'Hare had fishing waters along that stretch of river. He also owned and operated the Doctor's Island fishing camp in Blackville. As a teenager, I slept on the rock for at least two falls while working as his guide.

Paul resembled Groucho Marx and came from New York City during the late 1930s, fishing with his first wife in the Doaktown area. In 1941 they bought Doctor's Island from Alfred Underhill, who had acquired it from Archie Alcorn during Alcorn's bankruptcy. Underhill had been using the island as a cow pasture. (The original owner, however, was a Dr. Idare from New England, who gave the island its name before the turn of the century.) Paul and his wife hired Jim and Max Gillespie to cut logs and raft them down the river to the island where Frank Mountain, an expert cabin builder, built the main lodges at the top of the island facing upstream.

Paul smoked a straight-stemmed pipe, like Mark Trail, wore plaid shirts and was a colourful figure in the Miramichi for years. He also owned a farm in Derby, and in the winter, ran a power-saw sales-and-service shop with the assistance of Lloyd Sturgeon, one of his early guides. Lloyd had a motorcycle accident on April 9, 1951, and lost a leg. He never guided much after that, but was an excellent outboard motor and power-saw mechanic.

Lloyd was the most knowledgeable fly-fisherman and the best caster I ever knew. After the accident, he taught my brother Winston and me how to cast a fly so it would light on the water and move as softly as a natural insect. We hooked our first salmon that summer of 1951 when I was eight. Lloyd also taught us the principles of the internal-combustion engine: spark and explosion.

I was still under age when I started guiding for Paul in 1960. It was my first job away from home. I can still remember taking the Bible in my hand and being sworn in as a guide by Blackville game warden Al Lebans. Mr.

Lebans chewed tobacco and added the words, "And are you positive you're 18?" to the oath. I was small but Mr. Lebans knew I had grown up around the sports.

Paul's foreman at the time was Max Vickers, and Max was very good to my brother Winston (Paul called him Win) and me. We joined Paul's team of guides along with Stafford and Norm Vickers (brothers to Max), Clarence Mountain and Gordon Munn. In Win's and my age group were Paul Gillespie and Alvin Harris.

Paul had many friends from the New York area who came to camp regularly. Dr. John Losier, a dentist from Lyndhurst, New Jersey, was one of them. Others were Sye Diamond, Guthery Cunningham, Colonel Poole, Aberly and Webb, Mack Mills and Danny O'Hare (Paul's brother.) It was also here that Ted Williams of the Boston Red Sox came to fish.

I guided Dr. Losier for two falls, and Win guided him for years after that. Dr. Losier was an excellent angler and had fished with Lee Wulff on the Four Toe River in Labrador. He certainly didn't need me to show him what to do, so my job was easy. He have me a pack of Camel cigarettes each morning, and because he loved the Gray Rapid pool, we went there. I slept on the big rock while he fished.

Because Ted Williams was around, there was word that, possibly, Joe Di-Maggio was also. Following this, there was always the rumour that Marilyn Munroe was in camp. I've since talked to an old-timer from the rapids who claimed to have guided the beautiful blonde. We were always looking for her to come out of a camp. If we saw a woman at some distance away on the river, for a moment, it was Marilyn. To me, then and still, any woman on the river is a beautiful sight. But Marilyn . . .

Anyway, all of this gave the whole operation a touch of romance. I have heard all my life that Marilyn Munroe fished here, and I don't know for sure that she didn't . . . but she was here that fall, in spirit at least, and in the minds of us who watched for her.

I had a girlfriend in Blackville at the time, my first love. On those yellow and breezy September days, as I lay on the rock watching Dr. Losier fish, I would think of her and of when I could get off to go and see her. I thought about Marilyn too, and somehow, to me, the two women started to look alike. I loved both women equally and both were equally elusive.

Other celebrities rumoured to be fishing on the Miramichi were the actors Vince Edwards, and years later, Tom Selleck who was reported to have bought out Ted Williams. The only real celebrities that I knew to fish here were, in fact, Ted Williams and his friend, boxer Jack Sharkie. Writer and film personality Lee Wulff fished here many times, as did musician Hoagie Carmichael in 1986. General James Doolittle and Stillman Rockefeller stayed at Wade's fishing camp in Howards in the 1950s.

One day, when I was reclining on Liar's Rock and my mind was somewhere else, I heard a splash and shout, and rose to see the doctor submerged with only his head out of the water. I scampered into the cold river without waders and assisted him, coughing and sloshing, to shore. He had slipped on a rock and lost his balance. Afterwards, I waded in and retrieved his Thomas rod, glasses and drifting fly box. I can still recall drying Dr. Losier's roll of grey $20 bills, spreading them out around the circle of the fire. The following morning, when I arrived for work in long chest waders, Paul O'Hare and Dr. Losier laughed for an hour. They always teased each other in such cases, reminding me of Abbot and Costello or the Marx Brothers.

But on the river, Dr. Losier was serious. He fished hard, and he loved barbecued salmon. Each day before noon, my job was to gather hardwood and build a fire. From the camp we took only bread, tea and a grill. When he caught the first grilse of the morning he would ask me to cook it for lunch.

I would split the grilse up the belly and open it up flat like a snowshoe. Then I would lay it in the grill, flesh-side down, over the hardwood coals. After 20 minutes, the leaves of the fish started to curl and it would be turned over and held, skin side to the coals, and scorched so the skin would come off in one piece to be thrown away. Then the backbone was removed, leaving only two pink slabs of salmon, which we ate with homemade bread and 10-minute-boiled-river-water tea.

I will always be grateful to Dr. Losier for teaching me how to cook a salmon on an open fire. He always emphasized how important it was to use hardwood and not charcoal or gas for cooking salmon, and to cook the fish flesh-side down as all the fat was in the skin and would drip through and keep the fish moist. I have cooked many salmon like this since, always with positive comment. Dr. Losier became a friend of my family and we corresponded for many years afterwards. When Paul sold Doctor's Island some years later, and moved to Montana, Losier fished at the Wilson's camp in McNamee.

Even today, when I'm barbecuing a salmon at my cabin, the scent of the fish, the hardwood fire and the bush tea are reminders of those days when the cool September winds pushed up the river and the yellowing sun tried to warm me from those autumn blues at Liar's Rock.

It comes back to me, too, when I smell the smoke of an American cigarette (we didn't know that smoking was bad for us then, and considered it to be romantic), or hear a song by Peter, Paul and Mary or the Highwaymen. I think of how I could once glance across the river to watch the great Ted Williams, then a man in his 40s, casting a long and perfect line. Below him would be Jack Sullivan, the flamboyant outfitter from Blissfield, with a guest or two. And there was always a blonde-haired beauty in the pool (she could have been with Ted or Jack) throwing a decent line. They'd shout to each other above the din of the water that bubbled around the waders. The constant upriver wind would toss the waves and put the whole scene in motion.

And the women, God bless them, from a distance, were always Marilyn Munroe.

Wayne Curtis is a freelance writer and author of *Currents In The Stream, One Indian Summer, Fishing The Miramichi* and *The Growing Seasons*. He lives in Newcastle, New Brunswick.